Inventing a
Once in a While the Odd Thing Happens, The Blue Ball

Paul Godfrey is part poet, part philosopher and most excitingly very much part dramatist. *Guardian*

Inventing a New Colour, what starts out as a domestic drama, ends up as a poetic elegy for the world before war. *Financial Times*

A Bucket of Eels is an apocalyptic contemporary farce, tracing a series of bizarre events unleashed when a bridegroom runs away on the eve of his marriage.

Once in a While the Odd Thing Happens . . . A series of delicate verbal ballets played out against the wild Suffolk landscape . . . the play's images linger in the mind. *Time Out*

The Blue Ball a National Theatre commission which launched Paul Godfrey into orbit to probe the dark side of Cape Canaveral and Kzakhstan's Star City in a renewed assault on the mysteries of the universe. *Independent on Sunday*

Paul Godfrey was born in the West of England and trained as a director in the Scottish Theatre. His work includes *Inventing a New Colour* (Royal Court, Bristol Old Vic), *A Bucket of Eels* (RSC Festival: The Other Place, BT Connections Scheme: Royal National Theatre), *Once in a While the Odd Thing Happens* (Royal National Theatre), *The Panic*, libretto to a score by David Sawer (Royal Opera House Garden Venture), *The Blue Ball* (Royal National Theatre), *Trilogy of New Plays from Different Sources: The Modern Husband* (Actors' Touring Company), *The Invisible Woman* (The Gate), *The Candidate* (Royal Exchange Theatre, Manchester), and *Catalogue of Misunderstanding*.

PAUL GODFREY

Plays: 1

Inventing a New Colour
A Bucket of Eels
Once in a While the Odd Thing Happens
The Blue Ball

introduced by the author

Methuen Drama

METHUEN CONTEMPORARY DRAMATISTS

2 4 6 8 10 9 7 5 3 1

This collection first published in Great Britain 1998
by Methuen Drama, Random House, 20 Vauxhall Bridge Road,
London SW1V 2SA

Random House Australia (Pty) Limited
20 Alfred Street, Milsons Point, Sydney, New South Wales 2061, Australia

Random House, New Zealand Limited
18 Poland Road, Glenfield, Auckland 10, New Zealand

Random House South Africa (Pty) Limited
Endulini, 5A Jubilee Road, Parktown 2193, South Africa

Inventing a New Colour first published by Nick Hern Books in 1988.
Copyright © 1988 by Paul Godfrey
Once in a While the Odd Thing Happens first published by Methuen in 1990
Copyright © 1990 by Paul Godfrey
A Bucket of Eels first published by Methuen in 1995.
Copyright © 1995 by Paul Godfrey
The Blue Ball first published by Methuen in 1995.
Copyright © 1995 by Paul Godfrey

This collection copyright © 1998 by Methuen
Introduction copyright © 1998 by Paul Godfrey
The right of Paul Godfrey to be identified as the author of this work has been
asserted by him in accordance with the Copyright, Designs and Patents Act, 1988

A CIP catalogue record for this book is available from the British Library

Papers used by Random House UK are natural, recyclable products made from
wood grown in sustainable forests. The manufacturing processes conform to the
environmental regulations of the country of origin.

ISBN 0–413–71880–8

Random House UK Limited Reg. No. 954009

Typeset by Deltatype Ltd, Birkenhead, Merseyside
Printed and bound in Great Britain by Cox & Wyman Ltd, Reading, Berkshire

Contents

Paul Godfrey
A Chronology

1987   Completed *Inventing a New Colour*.
        Left Scotland and moved to London.
        Wrote *A Bucket of Eels*.

1988   National Theatre Studio production of *Inventing a New
        Colour*, directed by Tim Supple.
        Royal Court/Bristol Old Vic co-production of *Inventing
        a New Colour* directed by Phyllida Lloyd.

1989   Completed *Once in a While the Odd Thing Happens* and
        directed National Theatre Studio production.

1990   Directed Royal National Theatre production of *Once in
        a While the Odd Thing Happens* in the Cottesloe Theatre.
        Began to write *The Blue Ball*. Visited NASA, Lyndon
        Johnson Space Centre, Houston.

1991   Wrote libretto for David Sawer's opera *The Panic*,
        produced by Royal Opera House Garden Venture.
        Wrote replies to Shakespeare's sonnets for a
        collaboration with Shared Experience Theatre.
        Visisted NASA, Cape Canaveral, Florida.
        Directed revival of *Inventing a New Colour*, Northcott
        Theatre, Exeter.
        Visited Russian Space Programme, Star City, Moscow.

1993   Completed *The Blue Ball*.
        Began *Trilogy of New Plays from Different Sources* by writing
        The Modern Husband (inspired by Henry Fielding).

1994   RSC Festival production of *A Bucket of Eels*, The Other
        Place, Stratford-upon-Avon.
        Delivered lecture to Royal Court Writers' group; *A
        Handful of Water: the present moment in British playwriting*.
        Wrote *The Candidate* (inspired by Gustave Flaubert).

1995   Delivered lecture to British American Arts Association
        conference, South Bank Centre; *The Artist and the
        Institution: The Playwright and The Theatre*.
        Directed the Royal National Theatre production of
        The Blue Ball, Cottesloe Theatre.

National Theatre BT Connections Scheme produce *A Bucket of Eels* nation-wide and in Cottesloe.
Actors' Touring Company production of *The Modern Husband*, directed by Nick Philippou, national tour and Lyric Hammersmith, London.

1996   Completed *The Invisible Woman*, (inspired by Terence Afer), and co-directed, with Ramin Gray, production at the Gate Theatre, London.

1997   Royal Exchange, Manchester production of *The Candidate* directed by Braham Murray.
Completed *Catalogue of Misunderstanding*.

Introduction

One Playwright's Beginning

This volume contains the first plays I wrote in the order I wrote them. Here are seven years of writing. As I wrote I discovered what I was doing and as I wrote it changed. Now I realise these are the plays that made me a playwright.

When I began I had no idea where it might lead. It was a simple ambition to write a play in the hope it would be staged. Then once I had completed a play I wanted to write a different one. Consistently this desire has returned to me, and with each play I have aspired to stretch my imagination and examine the possibilities of playwriting differently.

No play that I have written has ever turned out as I expected. There's a constant disparity between the play I think I am writing and the play I actually write. I know what I am doing yet I am surprised by the work itself. So as long as this disparity exists to fuel my curiosity I shall continue to write.

I have always written to the moment and sought to witness the experience of living now. Thus it is a curious sensation to gather these four plays here, recognise this as the end of one process and equally as the beginning of another, without limit. I used to put these plays in envelopes and address them to theatres but this is where I send them off without addresses. Who knows all the places, where and when, they may arrive?

No one can say where a play finds its true audience. I have learnt that it is arbitrary whether the work of a particular playwright should meet the taste of a theatre culture at any given moment. Think of poor William Congreve who gave up after the failure of *The Way of the World* or Georg Büchner who never had any of his plays produced in his lifetime. It is not modesty when I count my own good fortune that I have seen all the plays I have written reach the stage.

There's no doubt writing plays for the theatre is a rare employment. For more than ten years I have made my living by it and I can count on the fingers of one hand those of my contemporaries who do this as their central occupation. It seems our theatre can only sustain a small number of playwrights. In spite of the strong rhetoric of encouragement and the nurturing of new playwrights, the reality of making a living or creating a range of work beyond a couple of plays remains elusive.

When the majority of writers who start in theatre move into TV it creates an atmosphere in which the formal distinction between writing for these different media is not always apparent. So why did I continue writing for theatre when TV might have given me a more reliable income through this time? I continued because I had enough productions of my plays to live, and I won some awards. I continued because each time I finished a play I began another and then I concentrated solely on completing that. I continued because (unlike actors and directors who need each other to work) as a writer no one can take the paper from your hand. I was able to use time as I chose. Somehow I learnt the knack of survival and the more I wrote the more engaged I became in pursuing the writing that is distinct to theatre.

Before I began to write I had worked as a director in the theatre for five years when I recognised an urge to get out into the world. I wanted to confront myself but whether writing was the outcome or source of this I cannot tell. The reasons I began to write are inextricable from why I wrote my first play *Inventing a New Colour* and this is one of the ways I understand that title.

I was of the first generation of my family to receive the privilege of higher education and it was a bad experience for me. It took away my speech. In that environment I learnt to survive by talking other than I had grown up to speak. Though I could still hear it in my head you might say I had it knocked out of me. Then I felt cheated and disorientated, and it was out of a need to repair this feeling that I wrote my first play. I became conscious of a whole world behind me and of the rich culture I'd been born into. By writing a play I could interact imaginatively with this world of which I am no longer a part. I projected the drama into the recent past, before my birth, to understand how that world came to be as I discovered it. The play is set in the cathedral city where I was born and in my play it is the centre of the world.

Too often in drama the speech of the English regions, and of the West Country in particular, is used to signify stupidity or a comic character. Only rarely have I seen it used to convey reality. I wrote my first play in this speech, gave my protagonists large experiences and allowed them to be articulate in their own words. On the outskirts of my home town there's a theatre built as part of the enlightened post-war repertory movement. When I wrote my play this theatre had existed for twenty years and no actor had even spoken on the stage as people do in the town. I imagined achieving this would be the culmination of my quest but when I submitted my play to the theatre they rejected it outright.

Here I confronted a central reality of any playwright's existence which is that whatever you may create in your imagination it cannot exist publicly without the complicity of a theatre to stage your play. Over the following months I received refusals from other regional theatres until eventually I had only the London theatres left and I submitted the play there with little expectation.

Inventing A New Colour was taken from the post bag and produced by the Royal Court Theatre. It changed my life when they selected the play from the thousands they receive and wrote back to me. That day I was woken by the letter thrown down onto the bed and the physical memory of this remains vivid to me now. I opened my eyes to a small envelope franked Royal Court. This was my first good response and they asked me to call as soon as possible. Then while I was out at that meeting with the Royal Court someone rang me at home from the National Theatre. It was the same story there. This was a moment in my life. Both theatres were interested in the play and I was presented with a choice. The outcome was a production without decor, in private, at the newly created National Theatre Studio in Waterloo and a subsequent co-production between the Royal Court and the Bristol Old Vic in the same year. After the play had won recognition in the metropolis I was asked to direct a revival at the theatre in the town where it is set.

My relationship to the world was altered by these events. Once I discovered what writing could do I no longer had any feeling of being cheated. I had some orientation now and I had a lot of ideas too. From this moment playwriting became my life.

Inventing a New Colour was written in Scotland and I came south with it, then after six months searching I found somewhere to live in London. I rented a room in a riverfront house in West London. My outlook was an expanse of water and when high tide brought the Thames up to the front door we had to go in and out by the back gate. Here I settled down to write another play.

This was a time when many of my contemporaries were getting married. Each striving to reconcile their own wishes with the possibilities of fulfilment that were available to them. Attendant upon their expectations was the search for stable employment and the creation of an adequate household. It was a brave gamble that many undertook.

Out of this came *A Bucket of Eels*. The drama is contemporary and describes a specific modern society yet the play has a classical form. I wanted to release my characters from a naturalistic world into a larger universe that contained poetry and even magic. For me contemporary playwriting is not an epilogue or an addendum to European drama but a continuum with the work of the last five hundred years. The education I received gave me a wide knowledge of playwriting in English. When I came to compose *A Bucket of Eels* as a classical play I met my playwriting antecedents.

As a playwright I perceive the world through dialogue, I am aware that the stresses of a society are visible in the relationship between couples. Twins and pairs in opposition are essential motifs in classical drama but while *A Bucket of Eels* contains these figures there's nothing systematic in the play. Each of my characters traces the successes and failures of an individual as he or she struggles to recognise their desires and match them with the options they discover as a result. Something that defines the drama of our lives for each one of us.

This play found its moment when it received a spate of productions nation-wide performed by young actors as part of a National Theatre Education scheme. The delight in seeing these performances was that in each place the actors spoke in their own voices and in each instance these distinctive ways of speaking revealed different aspects of the play just as each of those places locates itself differently within the culture.

Once I'd sat in a room and written two plays it was time to use playwriting to get out of it. Now I chose a real story that I was able to explore for myself from the living memories of whoever I could track down. My awareness was filled with how to survive as a playwright. What does it mean when writing plays is your contribution to existence? These were years when the necessity of art was questioned and artists were expected to have justifications for the value of their work. This situation struck a chord for me with the story of Benjamin Britten writing the first grand opera in English during the Second World War. He was hated for a contrary act in a society directed solely to war. There was no justification except that *Peter Grimes* exists as the only English opera to enter the world repertoire and its appearance became part of the post-war cultural rebirth.

I was attracted by the force and beauty of Britten's music. Researching *Once in a While the Odd Thing Happens* took me into that world and the stories I heard evoked powerful characters. There was an obvious drama in the existence of Benjamin Britten and Peter Pears as the first visible homosexual couple to gain any acceptance in modern British society. Later when the play was staged by the Royal National Theatre coincident with the Government's Clause 28 Legislation this was described by a professor from Columbia University in a critical work as 'a page in gay history'.

Any playwright wants an audience to accept their play as real, something true, and I quickly realised the power of manipulating facts within my fiction. In creating a fiction from a real story I was aware of exploring an ambiguous area in which fact may not be truth and truth may no be factual. I believe good fiction is truth. The research propelled my imagination into a world beyond my own experience. It was never just biographical and though people recognised the characters in the play as portraits, I know they are figures I created. History provided a specific story that enabled me to construct a drama for its own resonance. No pre-knowledge of these people is required to understand it.

Once in a While the Odd Thing Happens was the first play of mine I directed. I've had good experiences when other people have directed my work but now I had the pleasure of choosing who I wanted to cast. By working closely with these gifted and responsive actors I learnt more about the potential of my language and play writing than I had seen before. We were a concentrated team and we had joy working together. This was an experience that remains an inspiration to me. Initially we rehearsed the play at the National Theatre Studio and it became one of the first pieces of work to travel from the Studio into the main repertoire of the Theatre.

Then with the option to write another play for the Royal National Theatre I chose to challenge everything I had learnt and take a huge leap into the dark. Perhaps I wouldn't have undertaken the enterprise if I had known it would take three years to complete this play but it was the right moment to seize an extravagant imaginative ambition.

I was a child when I saw the first human step on to the moon yet it had no larger significance for me beyond our immediate domestic world. Born six months before Yuri Gagarin became the first human in space, I was an unwitting child of this space age. It fascinates me that an experience as wondrous as our first forays into space could have been rendered mundane in such a short time and I wanted to explore how this paradox could be. So I set out to meet astronauts. I applied for a writer's grant to visit America and with the name of the Royal National Theatre behind me I negotiated my way into NASA. Subsequently this led me to visit cosmonauts in the Russian Space programme where I found myself also witness to the end of the Soviet Union. Returning from Moscow I moved out of West London and set up a writing studio in Clerkenwell at the heart of the city where I undertook the task of using playwriting to embrace this extraordinary experience.

In total perhaps I spoke to twenty-five astronauts and cosmonauts. They were as different as twenty-five people could be and these differences could not be said to fall into any pattern that reflects the differences of east and west. For people living and working within a space programme there is a specific common experience that exists independent of national identity. I found it possible, using my own language, to create scenes and characters in a space programme that explore this experience. Scenes informed equally by my knowledge of both programmes.

If you ask an American who was the first in space they will

say either Alan Shepard (the first above the earth's atmosphere) or John Glenn (the first to orbit the earth), they will be unlikely to say Yuri Gagarin (the first of all). The first human in space is already a figure of mythology and in the play I call him Alex.

Dealing with a subject that engenders disbelief I needed a bridge to bring the audience to it. So the play contains scenes of research with a character who has my name. While I want an audience to accept these scenes as real let me admit they are inspired by my experience and not an account of it. They were created to serve the play. If I hadn't done the research I couldn't have written this play, or rather, not *this* play. Here are events that happened, that might have happened and some that didn't.

Completing *The Blue Ball* was a watershed and when I had achieved it I found seven years had passed, as if overnight, since I began my first play. It was an eventful journey. Over this time I began to know other playwrights whose early work had also been presented at the Royal Court. In the years between completing *The Blue Ball* and the production of the play at the Royal National Theatre I came to know them better. While at first the factionalism of British theatre at that point appeared to divide us and while the presence of limited production opportunities appeared to place us in competition for the same spaces, once we got to know each other we found we had more in common as playwrights than the things that might keep us apart. Around a dozen of us from the Royal Court Writers' Group met in private to discuss what we could do to improve the situation of playwrights within the theatre. Through conversation we learnt that many of the individual struggles we'd had and understood as reflections of ourselves and our work were common experiences and reflections instead of the theatre culture.

I remember Winsome Pinnock said that if we could not collaborate in a shared action we would not exist as a generation. To the meeting of playwrights Gregory Motton brought a letter that he'd drafted. Together we hatched a plan to send this letter to each theatre in the country. The letter asked those theatres in receipt of subsidy if they could produce three new plays a year. Such an outcome would enliven the repertoire of these buildings, multiply the opportunities for playwrights and we believed it would transform our theatre culture. Not that we had any real expectation of this happening but we were attracted by the irony of the action itself. It was a serious and politely worded request and we hoped that people would ask why we had undertaken such an act.

Eighty-seven playwrights signed the letter and in collaboration with Sarah Daniels, Charlotte Keatley, Gregory Motton and Winsome Pinnock I was at the centre of the negotiations as we arrived at a mutually acceptable text. The letter was faxed to the newspapers on the day before it arrived at the theatres so that the question we posed would become one of public debate. It did, and for the first time in memory theatre was on the front page. Ultimately the letter became a collective statement by all the signatories. As playwrights we were delighted to have orchestrated the drama and retained our invisibility.

As we expected, our media intervention changed nothing. The great majority of theatres never replied and a half dozen merely acknowledged the letter's receipt. In spite of the international calibre of those playwrights who signed, the regional theatres could only respond with indifference. I value what we did because it was a noble gesture from which we gained nothing personally. It was the only action that ever brought so many playwrights of different demoninations into collaboration. For a moment we existed as a generation. It was a moment that revealed the truth of the position of the art of playwriting within our general theatre culture by contrast with the number of accomplished playwrights writing. Beyond that moment we proceed as individuals in our diverse ways but we did this one thing together. None of us who were directly involved has written of this before and I have done so because it is a moment I choose to remember.

Here you have an account of how I understand what I was doing in the seven years spanned by this volume. This is a retrospective testimony and space obliges me to tell the simple story here so I hope I have not given the impression that it was plain sailing for me or that I struggled exceptionally either. Both are untrue. Mikhail Bulgakov's novel *Black Snow* stands as the best account of the complex relationship a playwright enjoys with the theatre. My experience was not so different, and since I began by working on the staff of a theatre I have known each side of it.

If I used research to expand my horizons each of these plays is drawn from the imagination as much as from experience. I learnt about life through writing about it. The plays you have here are the most vivid expression of which I am capable of my central passions and concerns over this time. In my opinion the most interesting plays are not *about* what they're about, content and subject rarely coincide, so I must leave you to your own conclusions but I hope you will find something here that you recognise.

I loved writing these plays and I'd like to think that the equal measure of success and disappointment I found in these years stabilised me, not so much of either to discourage me from moving on, enough of each to allow me a sense of proportion. I followed the writing where it led me. I wrote the plays I could write and the plays I needed to write and in turn they gave birth to those that have come since.

I write a play to discover what it is, so if I already know what I want to say I shouldn't write the play. Equally if I could express what I want to express in another form I wouldn't write a play.

Emotions by their nature are ambiguous and thoughts are never simple. It is language that crystalizes our experience and theatre allows us to explore consciousness in a complex way. I know that an actor's response to a playwright's words, and an audience's perception of that in a moment, has the power to transcend the more reductive languages we use to describe ourselves as human. When I look at a play I am curious to discern what view of humanity is revealed by it. This is how theatre can remind us that we live in a larger world than it may sometimes appear to us.

The work and the life I created were the result of a series of choices I've outlined here. I might have chosen otherwise or the outcome of my choices might have been different. None of this matters any more because now these four plays exist independent of me, and this is how it happened.

Paul Godfrey
Clerkenwell, London
1998

Inventing a New Colour

Characters

June, *Eric's wife, working as a librarian*
Eric, *June's husband, working as an engineer*
Francis, *June and Eric's son*
Peter, *an evacuee*

Exeter, the Spring and Summer of 1942.

Set the action against a background indicating landscape with bands of colour: greens, greys, blues and browns.

While the play is set in the past, the period needs to be shown barely, it is that moment as if now.

The play was given a private performance at the National Theatre Studio on 29 April 1988, with the following cast:

June	Lynn Farleigh
Eric	Peter Needham
Francis	Peter Darling
Peter	Simon Gregor

Directed by Tim Supple
Designed by Moggie Douglas

First public performance at the Bristol Old Vic Theatre on 26 October 1988, and subsequently at the Royal Court Theatre in November that year, in a co-production between the two theatres, with the following cast:

June	Valerie Lilley
Eric	Sam Kelly
Francis	Nicholas Hewetson
Peter	Simon Gregor

Directed by Phyllida Lloyd
Designed by Anabel Temple

Act One

1

June
I look out from here
and I see the line of hills
beyond that another
and beyond that
mist.

There is not anywhere
here in this city
that you cannot see the hills
and I know
that is the quality of this place.

A city in the country.

Neither forgets either.

To be here is to see more.

Even our devastation is hemmed by fields.

2

Eric
When I was courting your mother
I used to wear wide turn-ups
and once
we'd been out
courting in the bracken
and I noticed
that one of my turn-ups was heavy.

Then when I got back
a green snake fell – bang –
on to the kitchen floor
and whipped away under the sink.

You can imagine my mother
'How did that get there?' she said

'been lying down?'

3

Francis
At school
I was told to paint the view
from my bedroom window

and I painted a dull green square
that filled the paper

with a smaller grey rectangle
that was the step down.

Other pictures were different,
the views you would see looking out.

I mixed and remixed that paint
'til it flaked off.

4

June
There is no clock in this house
that's the right time.

Eric sets the alarm a few minutes ahead
now and then
so he'll think he's late for work
and gain time in the morning.

Sometimes he alters the others
but I'm not certain which
neither is Eric, I think.

We still get to work though.

5

Kitchen: February.
Francis *comes in.*

Peter *is waiting. He has his things.*

Francis
Is this you, just arrived then?
Peter. The evacuee.

Peter
Me. Yes. Here,
here in the country.

Francis
Oh.

Peter
So much green here.
It's all green the countryside round here, isn't it?

Francis
Exeter's not exactly like that.

Peter
Ah, but Exeter's so old.

Francis
What's left.

Peter
My father said it was a place to have property, Devon.
I'd really like to have property round here.

Francis
Why here? When you've come from London.

Peter
I mean to retire to,
I'd give anything to be rich enough to retire down here.

Francis
It's damp you know here.
If you retired here you'd die of rheumatism.
Wettest valley in England, brilliant place to retire to this.

Peter
I was told we have to go and work in the fields out of term.

Francis
Yes.
We can walk back each day though, or cycle, along the canal.

Peter
There's no tram?

Francis
Look, I'd better tell you now.
My parents they're at the funeral.
My grandmother she died this week.
You've not come to a happy house.

Peter
Should I do something?
What should I do?

Francis
Nothing, just don't worry if they act out of the ordinary
when they get back.

Peter
Oh dear.

Francis
It's all right, don't expect them to be normal that's all.

Peter
No one's parents are normal.
My mother she's Italian.

Francis
That must be strange.

Peter
It's difficult sometimes but I don't mind it.

Francis
Is that all you've brought?

Peter
Yes.

Francis
You've brought quite a lot with you.

Peter
I'm late, I should've registered by five.
Is that the time?

Francis
It'll do.

Peter
Perhaps I can do it tomorrow.

Francis
Would you like to see the river?

Peter
Why is it interesting?

Francis
There's a weir.

Peter
Oh I've seen that from the train.
Did she die in the bombing then your granny.
Was it a bomb?

Francis
Not a bomb, old age.
She wasn't bombed.
She was very old.
You shouldn't laugh.

Peter
You are.

Francis
She was my granny.
I cried earlier.
She was more than eighty.
On Monday my dad found her in bed asleep,
dead.

Peter
Where do I stay?

Francis
My father asked me to clear half of my room
and he's brought in another bed.
Yours is going to be the one under the window
and there's a desk
but you could use this table for your homework.

Peter
There's going to be a lot of that isn't there?

Francis
School certificates you mean.
Are you taking them too?

Peter
That's why they sent me.
I missed them last year.

Francis
But you look grown-up.
Too old to be an evacuee.

Peter
I'm only seventeen.
These exams are important.
Aren't you a bit young to be taking them?

Francis
I've been sixteen for a long time.
How many are you taking?

Peter
Six, six is all you'll ever need.
You?

Francis
Eleven: Maths, English, Language and Literature,
History, French, Latin, Greek, Chemistry and Physics.

Peter
That's only nine.

Francis
R.I. and Art too.

Peter
You're the smart one.
There's no straw in your hair.

Francis
The only way to face these things is head on.

Peter
What?
Exams.

Francis
Head on and by the throat!

Peter
Don't you know there's a war on?

Francis
Half measures is no good.
To the hilt or not at all.

Peter
But why condemn yourself to all this rubbish then?
Where does it get you?

Francis
You'll see.

Peter
When we get back to work?

Francis
When we get back to school.

Peter
Do you think I'll get on all right?

Francis
You will.

Peter
Now tell me your name.

Francis
Francis.

Peter
Francis: the original Devon pirate.

6

June
A woman came into the library today, she put the books on the counter and ran, she ran away. That's the fines you see. Perhaps one day there will be an amnesty.

If I can get this Library Association exam it puts me up a level and I may be able to keep my job if, when, the war ends.

It would mean no more stamping books at the desk too. My hands are black from that ink and the action has been mindless for months gone.

Take the book, turn the book, take the card, change the card, stamp the card, shut the book. Next book. Hand the pile back, library card on top.

I wish the Anglo-Saxon was not so difficult. We had to go to a once-only class in Bristol, and the man looked around the room and said 'There's someone here who'll know more about this than anyone else.' We were all silent and then he looked at me and said 'You, The Exeter Book, I expect you know all about it.'

I knew nothing.

That the earliest shreds of our poetry were recorded here in the cathedral library. I'd never heard mention. A thousand years sitting there, more, and it's been a beer mat and a cutting board and for lighting candles.

'Exeter people did that' he said 'to the earliest poems in the English language.'

Mid-afternoon I sit in the library annexe and I work on it.

Piecing one word with another, slowly.

Incomprehensible.

7

Kitchen:
June *is there,* **Eric** *has just arrived.*

Eric
There's a letter for Peter
come through the door just now
and caught open on the box.

June
Eric for God's sake don't read the boy's post.

Eric
I was just interested that's all.

June
You want to be careful he'll be here in a minute.

Eric *puts the letter on the table.*
Peter *comes in and looks.*

Peter
Hello Eric, June.

Eric
How are you boy?

Peter
I saw a cat roll in a puddle!

June
There's a letter for you from London.

Peter
At last!

Peter *goes out with the letter.*

Eric
Hah! Look at that.
Hidden that boy.

June
Not deep then?

Eric
How long's he been here? Three weeks
and he's like a bullet out of a gun,
and he's bright too.

Francis *comes in.*

Francis
Anything happen today?

June
No, just a letter for Peter.

Francis
What's the date?

June
Twelfth of March.

Francis
Wet enough. (*To* **Eric**.) Hello.

Eric
Just a minute, can you walk properly Francis?
Come on now, walk properly.

Francis
What?

Eric
Don't act up, stand straight
and just walk properly
so your mother and I can see you walk.

June
Put your shoulders down Francis.

Eric
Why do you have to make such a show of everything?

Francis
Why can't I be left alone?
I walk properly all right.
Don't I walk up and down that bloody road every day?

Peter *comes in.*

Francis
Eight years now, four times a day, twenty times a week,
more than two hundred and fifty times a term.

Peter
You talking again.

Francis
What's that?

Peter
Seven hundred and fifty times a year.

June
They say the whole of South Street went last night.

Francis
Oh it's all right though, that was only really old buildings.

Eric
One good thing, and I'll tell you something now.

There's not one in the West Quarter I wouldn't like to see gone.
Let's keep all that to your exams
and have a clean sweep of some of these old places.

June
I'd rather it didn't have to happen this way.

Eric (*to* **Francis**)
I don't see you so keen to refuse new boots when I offer them.
Happy enough to ditch old ones then.
What use old boots eh?

Francis
They say you can make soup out of old boots!

Eric
Don't talk soft boy.

Peter (*to* **Francis**)
I reckon they've given us six hours homework tonight.

Francis
That's what it's been every night this week
and I bet we'll need to carry on at this rate too.

June
You two boys are exam-crazed.
Who's best at this who's worst at that.
As if it was all that matters.

Francis
Don't you want us to get our exams?

Francis *walks out of the door and leaves it open.*

Eric
Door! Door!

Francis *comes in.*

Francis
Door! Table! Chair! Floor! Sink!

Francis *goes out.*

Eric
Shut the bloody door!

Peter *shuts the door.*

Peter
They were talking about Francis today at school, the
housemaster in the housemeeting this morning. He said 'There's
one boy in this school who I would describe as the most
aggressive boy here. That's Francis,' he said. And Francis grinned
and acted like he was hiding under the table. 'Yes I would have
no doubt in describing Francis as the most aggressive boy in this
school.' That's pretty amazing isn't it?

June
Francis will do all right
but he wants to watch his step at that school.

Eric
He acts far too clever when he'd do better to do what he was told.

Francis *comes in.*

Francis
What they tell me?

Eric
Don't you understand?
Why don't you do what they tell you?
You make life difficult for yourself.
Is it so difficult?

Francis
Why should I do what they tell me?
Not if I don't want to, not if I think they're wrong.

Eric
You think you know more than them, eh?

Francis
Yes, well, in fact I do about some things.

Eric
Well you're just iggerant then . . .

Francis
Iggerant? Ignorant!
Can't you even talk properly?

June
Can't you see that if you constantly do what they tell you not to,
people will dislike you.

Francis
Either you live by the rules other people set you
or you set your own.
I'm going to set my own.

Eric
Another day over!

Eric goes out.

Francis
Another day over!
Another year over!
Another meal over!
He says it all the time you know.

June
I know.

Francis
I don't think he even notices.
Another tea over!
Another journey over!

June
It's not stupidity you know or meek acceptance of other people's
rules, it's a satisfaction in what's complete, complete and
satisfactory. He'll say 'another job done', 'another row of potatoes
planted'. A pleasure in modest achievement not an all-suffering
ignorance.

'Another war over', that's what I want to hear right now.

Francis, I don't enjoy having you here criticising. I don't enjoy
hearing jibes at your father. Do you think he enjoys his only son
always out to attack or undermine him?

Peter doesn't enjoy being here.
You may be clever and don't we all know it.
We love you but we don't always like you.

Francis
You bore me.

June *goes out.*

Peter
Friday night, I wish we could go somewhere.
Hey, why *are* you taking all these exams?

Francis
Why?
So I can take higher school certificates, that's why.

Peter
I'd rather be out, out on the town,
up the West End, on the tiles, downing the beers!

Francis
I need them so I can go to university.

Peter
It's not my cup of tea.
But perhaps that's right for you.
You could do very well there.
You're lucky to be able to choose.

Francis
Why?

Peter
Why what? Why so bitter?
You could stop now.
Why take all these exams?

Francis
Why, because if we're forced to play this bloody game,
let's play it like a game, eh?

Peter
Fair dos for all? Or so that we can win?

Francis
Neither.
Let's throw the counters in the air
and let the people dive for them.
Sweep the board!
Change everything!

Peter
Oh Yes.
How?

8

June
Francis brought home a painting once
just before Christmas,
it was the three wise men
unfinished.
They were in a line,
red, orange and yellow,
with an incomplete background
in yellow also
which stopped when it reached the yellow one.

He asked me what to do
and I said
blend the colour to red
behind the yellow figure.

And the picture was a great success.

Three wise men coming
out of the rising sun.

9

Peter
I think I've arrived.

Three weeks and a bit and I think I am here now.

I know my way round.

This family, Francis and his mum and dad,
I feel they're my family now.

Though I'll be gone in the autumn, I know that too.

But while I'm here, it's as if I've always been here
now.

10

Eric
I was out early this morning
the world seemed glowing
green and white.
There was a mist and dew
which gave a shine to the leaves.
The river was grey
and the sky pale.

My mother is under the ground.

I stood and listened.

All the leaves heavy and shimmering.

Too much living and growing,
only so much soil,
only so much light,
leaf on leaf on leaf.

11

Kitchen: April.

June *writing, books open.*
Francis *comes in.*

Francis
They sent me home.

June *looks up.*

Francis
Hello.

June
What's wrong with you?

Francis
I broke my nose in hockey.

June
Oh no, not you Francis.

Francis
It doesn't hurt at all.

June
It looks all right anyway.
You're lucky to find me here, they changed the shifts,
so I'm working at home this afternoon,
on the Anglo-Saxon.

Francis
I did it in hockey.
A ball hit me, whack, and it's broken.

June
It's been here a thousand years that nose, you know
and you've broken it!

Francis
It wasn't my fault!
I was in goal and I defended by attacking
so he hit it right at me.

June
A Norman nose faced into the sea spray
and crossed the channel in history.
And you do this.

Francis
I cried.
'Quit snivelling' said the master and it's broken.
I've broken my nose.
Look at it.
'Quit snivelling'.

June
This nose pointed skywards, spanned the cathedral.

Francis
You do talk nonsense sometimes!

June
A hard look and a straight nose!

Francis
Straight nose! Ha! Ha!
If you asked me to follow it now I'd walk in a bloody circle.

June
Is there anything I can do for it?

Francis
They say I've not to touch it and it'll set straight on its own.

June
Not so bad for a boy.

Francis
That's all right then.

June
Was it Peter who hit the ball?

Francis
No. Might just as well have been though.
I expect he's still there battling up and down.

June
Why is it a battle?
You must be careful with him Francis.

Francis
I'm the one people have to be kind to.
I'm the one that's war-wounded!

June
That's not very funny just now.

Francis
Oh he's all right.

June
You know what I'm saying.

Francis
We get on.
What's this?

June
Still the Anglo-Saxon.

Francis
Is it interesting?

June
I don't know yet.

Your father says he wants you two boys to go out with him in the raids. Taking messages between the firewatchers.

Francis
How will we get our homework done?

June
If you sit down as soon as you get home you could do it then.

Francis
But when will I get a break?
When am I going to get some peace?

June
Think of everyone else.

Francis
I don't get much choice round here.
It won't make much difference to Peter though.
He doesn't do his homework most of the time.

Peter *comes in.*

Peter
Hello June.
Are you all right Francis?
I tried to come back with you but they wouldn't let me go.
What did the nurse say?

June
It's broken but it'll mend.

Peter
Hey it'll make you look really tough!
A broken nose.

Francis
Better than Pinocchio.

Peter
What's this you're doing?

June
It's Anglo-Saxon.

Peter
They didn't write very well.

June
That's just a facsimile of an original text.

Peter
What is it exactly?

June
It's riddles.
They're not comic though not jokes.
Would you like to look at one?
You have to imagine your own answers here.

She hands him a piece of paper. He looks up.

Peter
Shall we get our own tea then?

Francis
Mmmm I'm hungry too.

June
I'll do it for you.

Eric *comes in.*

Eric
What's wrong with you?

Francis
I'm waiting for my tea.

Peter
He's broken his nose.

Eric
Give the boy some tea Mother.

June
You're early too.

Eric
They shut the foundry
and as I'll be out tonight I knocked off.
No coal delivery this week at this time!
And I caught one of the apprentices at the canal.
He threw a machine part in the water.
He'd made it wrong, I could've milled it back again.
I felt sorry for the poor boy, he was so ashamed.

Just seventeen I think, same age as you Peter.

The following dialogues overlap.

Peter	Could I be apprenticed now then?
Francis	I've broken my nose.

June	You'd do better to get your school certificates.
Eric	Doesn't look serious to me.

Peter	But, I'm no good at them.
June	No one's to touch it.

Eric	Sciences will be useful.
Francis	What's this about messages?

Eric
They need some more boys to run messages between the firewatchers.

Francis
And you want us to do it?

Eric
Yes.

Peter
I wish I could be an apprentice,
doing something instead of this.

Eric
You could help me on the UXB's if you want.
I need a boy.
You'd have to keep right back while we did the defusing
but you could help move the pieces.

Francis
So I do the messages on my own?

Peter
Yes.
Eric, why did the boy throw the thing in the canal?

Eric
I only noticed because I used to do it myself, we all did. The apprentices have to make trial pieces and the materials cost money, now no one likes to admit their mistakes so they throw them away where nobody will know and they try again. There

must be thousands of machine parts in that canal.

June
One day they'll find them all.
God knows what people will think then!

12

Peter
It's cold this place.
Last night
in the shelter
it was wet.
I put my hand out to touch the mattress
and it was damp,
drops of water all over.
Every surface covered.

A wet hole in the ground.

It snowed on the sports field too
and nearly May.
Bare legs in the snow
and nearly May.

13

Eric
I went to the last war as
an engineer.
Fuel tanks I built underground
and I dismantled
simple explosive devices.
Now the war's here
with us.
So I go to people's gardens
and find incendiaries
like vegetable marrows.

I defuse them.

It's not safe.

Of course
I feel sorry for the boy,
Peter I mean.

14

Bedroom, late at night.
Francis *is still awake.*
Peter *comes in.*

Francis
You're late, the all-clear was hours ago.

Peter
They say it was the worst raid yet,
Eric sent me home,
he's still out.

Francis
How did you get on with him?

Peter
All right.
He's a good chap, I like him.
And I suppose I learnt a lot,
mechanical things, that'll be helpful in the Forces.
Some of the devices are quite simple.
Eric showed me one, it was just eight pieces.
I reckon I could take one apart in no time and rebuild it.
It'd not be difficult.
And they're not all big either.
I saw another
it would fit in my bicycle basket.

Francis
You know what your mother wrote?

Peter
You read my letter?

Francis
Yes. I found it.

Peter
Francis!

Francis
'I hope you had an uneventful journey.'
I can't understand how anyone can wish someone that.
It's too dull.
Life shouldn't be that dull.

Peter
I don't agree.

Francis
An uneventful journey.

Peter
How can you say that?
Christ, *four* raids this week.

Francis
Choose.
Choose now.
Eventful or uneventful.
I choose the profoundly eventful.

Peter
Oh Francis, just now: I'm away from home.
Bombs drop.
People die and kill.
My mother wished me an uneventful journey.
That's not unnatural.

Francis
But we have no choice, do we?

Peter
I try to get on with you, you know
but there you go acting up all the time.
I'm so tired. Tell me what you mean.
What do you *mean?*
You need to smarten up your ideas, Francis.

Francis
It's my house you live in.

Peter
Thanks, it's the middle of the night, that's marvellous.

Francis
I'm glad you're grateful City Boy.

Peter
Local yokel! Ha Ha Ha!

Francis
Goodnight!

Francis *goes to sleep.*

Peter
Francis wake up.

Francis *wakes up.*

Francis
I like the rustic impressions.
I mean what I say.
We have no uneventful journey.

Peter
Are we friends?
We are friends.
Aren't we?

Francis
Yes.
I think so.

Peter
It means a lot to me.
I've been very lonely
but if I know that you are my friend
then I can carry on and do it all
because I know you'll be there and I can talk to you.
Let's meet when we're old, shall we?
Will you come to my funeral if it's first?
I'll go to yours.

Francis
You are a fool.
I didn't know at all.

Peter
I'm sorry.

Francis
I was waiting for you.
Will you help me?

Peter
Yes of course.

Francis
It's serious.
You know you help my father now
to collect pieces of the dismantled UXB's.
I'd like to get enough pieces to make a bomb.
I'd like to blow up the school.
No more exams then!

Peter
That would be terrible.

Francis
I don't see.

Peter
Francis, some things are good and some bad,
everyone knows that.
This is *bad*!
Lots of people could be killed.

Francis
Not if we timed it right.

Peter
Buildings destroyed Francis.

Francis
That's the idea.

Peter
Why now?
Francis, making a bomb is *wrong*.

Francis
We go out and do it to the Germans.

Peter
That's very different.

The school is not our enemy, not like the Germans.

Francis
Oh yes?

Peter
Look we know we're right, on the side of good
but the Nazis are wrong.

Francis
Exactly.
The things we like and agree with are *good*
and those we dislike and disagree with are *bad*.
Got it?

Peter
It's not so simple.

Francis
Millions and millions of bombs drop every day,
yesterday, tomorrow.
How does one extra tip the balance.
Right or wrong?
We hate these exams, yes?
You do.

Peter
Yes.

Francis
Most of them will be no use.
You want to be a soldier, yes?

Peter
Yes, I suppose so.

Francis
And to me, well, they're a joke – a bad joke.
None of us knows why we go through this charade.
Who knows if the war will end even if we win.
So let's choose to sweep it all away.
You're not convinced.

Peter
People might be killed, you and me.

Francis
Look I've worked it out.
We assemble it under the stage in the hall
then we help to stack chairs one day
and stay to switch the lights off and one of us goes to set it.
After prayers the hall is always empty for an hour.
Peter no one will get hurt.
It's a miracle the school's not been hit already.
It's monstrous, how could they have missed?

Peter
Are you really serious?

Francis
I'm asking you to help me, as my friend, Peter.

Peter
Does this mean friends for ever then whatever happens?

Francis
Yes.

Peter
I'll go with you.

Francis
Everyone will be so sorry.
Poor boys, no exams.
Tragic, and they worked *so* hard.
Enforced school holiday.

Peter
How long have you been planning this?

Francis
How often will you go out with him on the defusing lark?

Peter
Three nights a week from now on perhaps.
As many nights as there are raids.

Francis
Can you start collecting pieces without him noticing?

Peter
Yes.

Francis
You and I.
Together.
Soon.

15

June
Mostly when I look at Eric
he's still the man I love.
He cuts his sandwiches at night,
hovers in the bathroom,
and lives in small ways.
Quite like a squirrel or a rabbit,
squirrel man.

The turn of his cheek,
line of his shoulder,
and shine in his eye,
that I love,
are not always there.

When Francis was four
he held his wrists together
comparing cuffs.

Eric does that and
I can not love him.

16

Francis
The high point of the week
that's Friday evening.
This is Sunday afternoon
the low.
Last week's homework is there.
Peter's gone out.
We've not talked about it,
bombs.
Everything goes on.

Bang!

I had a stupid idea,
there's not a chance it could happen.
No fear.
Not us.
Not for real.
Not at all.
Not here!

That's certain.

17

North transept Exeter Cathedral. The medieval clock is visible: April.
Eric *and* **June**.

Eric
Do you know what I saw?
Christmas trees, dozens of them, all dead and caught on the weir.
It's a bit late isn't it? I'll show you on the way back.

June
Do we need to walk that far in this weather?

Eric
There'd be no point in us going back the way we came June.

June
Can you hear the sleet on the boarding?
It's so dark with the windows gone from the cathedral.
It's a wonder this place is still here.

Eric
Sunday afternoon again.
Such a week it's been.
I wish I could be in the garden more.

June
Poor old dear man.
There's nothing we can do about the weather.

Eric
The weather is the least of it.
But I can't help thinking, there's such a lot to be done out there.

June
Now that you are out most nights,
you and I,
we have no time.

Eric
This is all we have.

June
And there's little to say.

Eric
There's nothing new at work.

June
I know.

Eric
Well you'd know because I'd tell you.

June
For a long time I thought I was unhappy
but now I think I am not.

Eric
Thinking yourself unhappy. That's really soft June.

June
Now I feel as if I'd only just woken up.

Eric
That's Sundays. We didn't get up till after eleven did we?

June
I was up earlier and left you to sleep you know.

Eric
I wish you'd stay with me when I'm asleep.

June
It's a blessing to sleep so long.

Eric
It's no skill.

June
Sometimes I'd like to sleep and not wake up.

Eric
Don't fall asleep now you've still got to walk home.
There's Peter.

Peter *has come in.*

Peter
Hello. How do you tell the time on this clock?

June
Hello Peter. I thought you were revising.
You've only got three weeks.
Peter you're soaked through.

Eric
I didn't expect to see you here.

Peter
You two went out.
Francis took his coat.
I wanted to come for a walk out as well.

Eric
Come on Mother tell us the time then.

June
You both have watches but since you ask:
The top dial shows the minutes, it's been added later,
and the outer ring on the main face shows the hours.
It's a quarter to four.

Peter
What about the inner rings?

June
In the centre, that's the earth, with the moon revolving.
It shows the days of the month and phases of the moon.
You can see the moon will be full at the end of next week.

Eric
That's what I don't want to see.

Peter
And the motto beneath.
What does that say?
'Pereunt et imputantur.'

June
It's Latin. I was told once, referring to the hours,
'They perish and are added to our account.'

Eric
I'd like to know all I've done in my time.

June
Is that what you think it means?

Peter
Do you know how this clock works exactly?

Eric
Electricity.

June
I'm cold. I'll sit by the heater at the west door and wait for you
two boys.

Eric
We'll light the fire when we get home June.

June
All right.

June *goes.*

Peter
Is June all right?

Eric
It's the moon.

Peter
Moon?

Eric
Bombers' moon.
The thought of more raids has upset her.

Peter
I see.

Eric
Looks like we'll be out most nights next week I'm afraid.

Peter
Just like last week?

Eric
Yes.

Peter
I don't mind.

Eric
Thank you Peter.
I've always wanted to say to Francis but couldn't,
so I'll say it to you, about June.
I've been lucky in love and I don't care who knows.

June and I, we've not always seen eye to eye, like now,
but who does?
I'll tell you I couldn't have asked better.

And this Anglo-Saxon it's useless probably,
even now, a waste of time but why shouldn't she do it?

She's an educated woman, my wife, you know.
Not like you and me,
of course that's who Francis takes after.

Peter
I'd noticed. That's why he beats me in arguments,
he knows more words. It's not fair.

Eric
Look before we go, see that window.
The stained glass in it had a panel of two boys fighting.
Just like you and him.

Peter
Was it old?

Eric
Oh yes there's always been two boys fighting!

Peter
Where is it now then?

Eric
Taken with the rest to be stored till after the war
against the bomb damage.

Peter
Francis and me, we're not going to fight any more.

18

June
I stood at the sink today
and before I washed it,
I held Peter's vest to my face
and I smelled his smell.

He's a year older than my boy
Francis.
Do we have children?
How is that one mine?
I wonder
what he tells me
how much is it?

These boys
we are theirs.

Peter's vest it was warm.
Francis wears two jumpers.

19

Eric
The boy is too keen
by half.

Then tonight
when the raid comes
he's not here.

I've seen him
up to something
taking things.

Is he safe?

The city
it's burning
and he's not here.

20

Peter
I never thought it.
I never expected it to work.
My God.
I slotted the metal pieces in place
and attached the detonator timer,
it moved.
I could have removed it
perhaps?
But I wasn't capable.
I sat
and looked at it.
I
did
it.
My God.

Act Two

1

Francis
My first memory of the Exe
was walking on it.

Next,
Summer
and paddling in the warm
I put my foot through a salmon
dead
and rotting in the mud.

Now
my mother says the word 'Exeter' means
'a river abounding in fish'.

Last year
when the weir dried
and salmon teemed in the pool
boys came with air rifles
shooting into the water.

Now they spray the river
on to the burning buildings
in Salmon Pool Lane.

The bombs leave us with ashes
and last night
our house was gone.

2

Allotment shed: Next day.
Peter *curled up.*
Francis *comes in.*

Francis
Hello Peter.
We thought we'd lost you.

Peter
How did you find me?

Francis
I knew you'd be here.

Peter
That easy?

Francis
Transparent.

Peter
What's happened?

Francis
You know.

Peter
What now then?

Francis
They're all upset, it's horrible.
We stay in a shelter tonight
and go to my grandmother's tomorrow.
It's miles out.
The house has not been touched since she died.
You must come.

Peter
Forget about me boy.

Francis
Well sir, since Hitler,
perhaps the only wholly evil man in the world,
dropped a bomb on Salmon Pool Lane,
you have nowhere else.

Peter
It wasn't Hitler's bomb.

Francis
What?

Peter
It was ours.

You know the pieces,
I put them together,
like your dad showed me.

Francis
In the house?

Peter
In the kitchen.

Francis
The kitchen!

Peter
During the raid.
And they worked, the last thing I expected.
The timer gave me thirty seconds and I ran.
I got your revision notes.

Peter hands them to **Francis**.
Francis takes the pile of papers and throws them on the ground.

Francis
Gone! All gone.
Whooah!
Rubbish house, room, street!
All gone!
Whooah!
No more exams, Peter!

Peter
We have to tell your parents you know.

Francis
No we must never do that.
No one must know.

Peter
But they're upset, it was their home.
They took me in, you're their son.

Francis
I'm still here.

Peter
How can we not tell?

Francis
Because it would make nothing easier.
Things would be more painful that way.

Peter
You're a coward.

Francis
This will be more difficult.
No one but you and me must ever know.

Peter
How can we go on as if we'd done nothing?
Won't they know, won't they guess something's up?
They know you too well, Francis.

Francis
Everything is different now we are no longer in that house.
All the changes in our behaviour, they will account to what's
happened.

Peter
I don't know if I can do this at all.

Francis
Look, I'll help you.
We're lucky not to be dead, if you are wise you will work as I
shall.
We have to keep doing the messages too.

Peter
You make it sound very easy.

Francis
Soon, you'll get your call-up. What?
Two and a half months, less.
That's what you want, isn't it?
You are not as tied as I am.

Peter
So we plug on and say nothing?

Francis
Yes.

Peter
I'll try Francis I promise you that.

Francis
Come on, let's go.

Peter
Your revision notes better take them.
We will still have to go to school, take exams.

Francis
Do you think so?

Peter
The school is still there.
What reason is there not to?
You said I should work as you will.
Isn't that what you meant?

Francis
I don't know.
I didn't think.

Peter
Not like you Francis.

Francis
You're not stupid Peter.
Did you take anything of yours when you left?

Peter
No, I don't care about that.
It's all a mess.
In London, my sister may be dead, my mother gone,
and I did this here.

Francis
It was our idea remember?
My fault as much as yours.
Perhaps our house would have gone anyway.

Peter
Perhaps?
Perhaps you're right

3

June
Eric keeps saying to me:
Nothing matters *that* much.
Nothing matters that much.
Nothing matters.

The saddest days of my life.

I go back to look.
I know there can be happier times
but when?
The work
and the discomfort of our lost home
envelop me.
Time will pass.
The Anglo-Saxon has all gone.
I'll forget that.

There's still our cathedral
almost untouched.
But I have no more words tonight.

4

Eric
I'm rubbing my finger and thumb
like this
and noticing it.

I have a half pint
and there I am
rubbing my finger and thumb
on the glass.

I pick up the paper
and I hear it,
the paper crackling,
and I see myself
rubbing my finger and thumb.

5

Francis
How do you paint the night indoors?
I used to lie planning it
part-closing my eyes
deciding the colours of the darkness.

I shut my eyes and see them.

I paint the powder paint on the sugar paper.
Colour and colour mixed in the pot,
greys streaked on the surface,
holes in the paper and drips on the floor.

I've tried now and used all the colours.
What next?

6

Eric's *mother's house: May.*
June *and* **Peter** *alone.*

June
What are you going to do tomorrow when the exams begin?

Peter
We've got to dig a trench all round the school so that we can
defend it if they invade. All of us not taking the exams will be
digging.

June
I've been wanting to talk to you about your future Peter.
I wish you'd not thrown away your chances of getting the
certificates. You see we feel a responsibility for you while you
are with us.

Peter
I wasn't as lucky as Francis was I?
I didn't have all the notes in my satchel that night.

June
All that work gone when you could have shared his books.

Peter
I've had enough sharing.

You know honestly it never was my strong point, exams.
What good do they do you when it comes to it?

June
Obviously exams only show who's good at exams
but people don't study simply for that.

Peter
None of this studying ever helps me to understand anything
either. It's only by doing that you find out.

June
And making mistakes?

Peter
Making mistakes, that's important too.
All these teachers, they've *taught* me all right
but what I've learnt,
I've learnt myself.
That's what I find.

June
Like my correspondence course for the library exam.

Peter
Yes, that's right, you have to work it out for yourself.

June
And when you have difficulty doing the exercises?
What then?

Peter
Then you invent the answers.

June
That's no good Peter.

Peter
Not unless they're right!

June
Then that's like cheating.

Peter
You won't invent the right answers
unless you understand the questions.

June
An educated guess.

Peter
Perhaps you can know more than you understand?
You can say more than you know.

June
If you took these exams you'd find you only knew what you
learnt.

Peter
I know more than I've learnt.
And I know what I want to learn.

June
But how is it you know what you want to learn, by reading?

Peter
Even reading though, it's all second hand isn't it?
The world at two removes.
My mother says it hurts your eyes . . .

June
. . . when you should be out in the fresh air?
You won't get much fresh air in the machine shop.

Peter
Look at him then, cooped up in that room, learning it all off
by heart and getting headaches and being sick.

June
I'm sure that's more to do with the broken nose.

Peter
He'll need spectacles next. Now that's really desperate.
No one's ever going to get me into a pair of them.

June
In the library I see hundreds of people come every day to
collect books from the shelves. At night they lie in the shelters
and read them. People need something like that to keep them
going.

Peter
Lucky we don't live in Germany where they burn the books
then.

June
What have you ever done?
There's such a lot you don't know.

Silence.

Peter
It's easy to say that. I could say it to you.

June
It's experience I'm talking about.

Peter
Quantity or quality, which is it counts there?

June
I don't think you understand what you're talking about.

Peter
I know what I'm saying.
Why did you give up your exam?

June
I don't know why I should tell you.
It wasn't because I lost my books.
It wasn't that at all. You don't get to read much at the issue
desk, and though I'll stay as long as I can, I've found that if
you love what's in the books, you don't work in a library.

Peter
What when you leave?

June
Perhaps I should be out in the fresh air.
There's a big enough garden.

Peter
This is more what I'd call country round here.

June
Eric grew up in this house. It's safer away from the city.

Peter
It's just far enough out of town to be able to get in.
Along the canal it's a good run.

June
You three go the same direction now.

Peter
Just till the end of term, Eric will be on his own then
when Francis and me have to go up the hill to the farm.
Can't imagine what that'll be like.

June
A couple of months farm work will do you no harm.

Peter
I'd like to go with Eric one day to the foundry.
At home I've seen the big machine shops in the dockland.
That's what I'd like to be, an engineer.
The Forces will get me my apprenticeship.
I'm keen to learn because I know I can do it you see.

June
I'm glad you know that at least.
If you get the chance I'm sure you'll do well.

Peter
You've been kind to me
and now I'm making the best of things until I go.

June
I'm sorry you've had such a miserable time with us.

Peter
Don't say sorry.
It's hardly your fault.

June
Francis told me what happened.

Silence.

Peter
Oh.

June
After the bomb.

Peter
Bomb?

June
After the bombs fell that night how he found you in the
allotment shed.

Why did you go there?

Peter
I was hungry,
I wanted to lie down,
that's all I could think.
I must have panicked in the raid that night.
I saw all the people leaving the city.

June
We thought we'd lost you.

Peter
I'm sorry.

June
There's something more isn't there?

Peter
No.

June
Sure?

Peter
What?

June
Tell me.

Silence.

Peter
I don't want to go you know.

June
Poor Peter.

Peter
At least Francis can think about his exams.
I've got nothing.

June
Seventeen and got nothing!

Peter
Please don't laugh at me.

June *kisses* **Peter**

June
No one's really laughing.

7

June
Today
when Eric didn't come
to meet me
I waited for the bus, not minutes,
two hours.
I could have walked in half an hour.
Everyone had gone,
I was still there
when it never came.

Now there's no study
I sit down to write
letters to everyone.
I think
most people spend their lives expecting to go on a journey.
I'll not drown in this
I walked home.

8

Eric
She took a great pride in the flowers my mother
and she did a big display at the end of the Great War.
In the final year she grew these tall blooms,
gladioli in golden colours
and all the same height.

Then when I came back
she borrowed my engineer's protractor to set them
at equal angles in wire.
It was to be a sunburst to go behind the altar.

When we got it there the angles were not so fine.

The sun burst skew-whiff behind the altar.

9

Eric's *mother's house: June.*
Peter *and* **Francis** *are sharing a bedroom. It is late.*

Peter
Last one tomorrow.

Francis
The last one for now.

Peter
How are you?

Francis
Terrible, stomach-ache.

Peter
When did it start?

Francis
In the afternoon.
I was sitting here revising when it began:
points of light, all colours and floating in space.

Peter
Like the flares falling.

Francis
It wasn't in the air though, this was just pinpoints of light.
I thought it was on the surface of my eyes, like dust.
I splashed my eyes in the sink.

Peter
Perhaps it was the heat?

Francis
I pulled the curtains against the light and it's gone.
Now there's this headache and my stomach, it hurts in pulses
and the ache keeps building up and fading.

Peter
The exams have not been that bad.

Francis
It was so hot this morning in History
I expected my hand to stick to the paper.

And I walked out and I thought that's that:
done History, forget History now.

Peter
So what have you been doing?

Francis
I've just been lying looking at the cracks in the ceiling.
Do you like this room?

Peter
I could be at home here.

Francis
No use feeling that if you're leaving.

Peter
I may not have a home when I get there.

Francis
Best to be at home in the world.
Then you'll be at home everywhere.

Peter
I like this house a lot even if it is run down.

Francis
This must be more what you imagined coming to the country.
Salmon Pool Lane was just the edge of the town.

Peter
It's so quiet here.

Francis
Quiet? Not completely quiet. Listen.

Peter *listens, then laughs.*

Peter
Apart from birds . . .
and the cows across the road
. . . and that tree, it's fairly quiet.
A lot quieter than my home.

Francis
Home?

Peter
London.

Francis
It must be very different.
I can't imagine you there.

Peter
Another world Francis.

Francis
I can't imagine it at all.

Peter
I'll be able to think of you here in this room in the country.

Francis
That's right, in the country bored to death,
in the country dying of boredom.

Peter
I think you should stay here.

Francis
But we all have to go away.
You just like it here because it's different.

Peter
Eric went away and came back.

Francis
Be like Eric, like him!

Peter
I don't see that would be so bad,
to be like your own father.

Francis
No fear!

Peter
Watch what you're saying, he's just out there creosoting the
fence.

Francis
Is that what the smell is?

Peter
Perhaps you should go then?

You are just like your father Francis.

Francis
Would you come back here?

Peter
I'd come for holidays and retiring.

Francis
Still on about that.

Peter
It happens to us all.

Francis
Like exams.

Peter
Not like exams.

Francis
My stomach it feels bad.

Peter *puts his hand on* **Francis***'s forehead.*

Peter
I wish I could make you well.

Francis *takes the hand and looks at it.*

Francis
There's dirt beneath your nails.

Peter
A lot of exams inside your head.

Francis
Your hands are filthy!

Peter
Dig in the day, dig in the night.
It's the story of my life these days.
Earthworks at school and gardening in the evenings.

Francis
Some city boy.

Peter
You know, even though we started so late here

Eric says the vegetables will be able to grow.

Francis
And your runner beans? How are they?

Peter
They'll be up the pole!

Francis
Perhaps you'll get to eat some before you leave?

Peter
Francis, why not go to sleep now?
You can't do any more tonight.
I'll test you when we walk up the road tomorrow.

Francis
Not long now.

Peter
Just tomorrow to get through.

Francis
Everything will be all right when the exams are over.
I can forget everything then.

Peter
Apart from what we did.

Francis
How do you mean?

Peter
A couple of weeks ago, I thought your mother knew.

Francis
I should have thought that had all settled by now.

Peter
It's been easier for you.

Francis
Leave it. It's all over Peter. Even the raids have stopped.

Peter
I'll never forget what I did.

Eric *has come in.*

Eric
You still worrying and moping about all that.

Silence.

(*To* **Peter**.) I'm going to be fair to you boy. Just a few kind words.
I'm going to say it in front of Francis too so there's no secrets.
Don't turn scared.
That night you never turned up, I went home to find you.

Peter
You knew where I was?

Eric
I knew you were too keen and I'd seen you taking those pieces. I guessed you were somewhere no one would go, larking about. Dangerous games, Peter.

Francis
What's this?

Eric (*to* **Francis**)
No doubt you were mixed up in this too.
God knows what you were up to exactly.
Something to do with that school I reckon.
Split them and sell them round the classrooms as trophies like shrapnel.
Was that it? Near enough the truth?

Silence.

I know you boys.

(*To* **Francis**.) Was this your daft idea?

Francis
What are you asking?

Peter (*to* **Francis**)
Can't you shut up!

Eric
I wouldn't trust either of you two.
You're lucky.
I'm not going to say anything to June about this.
We don't want to go upsetting your mother now.

And you
(*To* **Peter**.) can count yourself fortunate, you were nearly out
of the Forces, before you were in.
Now I'll not be able to trust you again Peter.
We don't talk about this, understood.
So you see I knew everything all along.
(*To* **Francis**.) Leave it Francis,
you can only do your best tomorrow.
You want to stop getting anxious about these exams.
You know your trouble boy?
You've got too much fear.

Eric *goes.*
Francis *retches.*

Francis
I'm going to be sick.

10

Francis
When I woke at five
the sun had risen.
Last day of exams.
Peter was asleep.
I stood in the glass house
still in nightclothes.
Eric's tomatoes were red
when I ate them.
And the migraine
gone.
I'd like to think
Peter made me well.
But the truth is
it's all gone.

11

Eric's *mother's house: August.*
June *is arranging lupins in a jar.*
Eric *watches.*

June
What happened to the summer?
That's what I keep asking myself.

Eric
I expect Francis ate it along with my tomatoes.

June
You'll get more tomatoes.

Eric
Those are lovely.
I don't remember them.

June
I found them in the garden.

Eric
Are they a new sort?

June
Just crossed in the wild I think.

Eric
What have you been doing?

June
Time to make a start I thought
so I've been doing some weeding in the front.

Eric
That's no way to do it.

June
It's a wilderness that patch.

Eric
She never touched it when she was on her own in the end.
We should start clean.

June
How are we going to do that?

Eric
Peter and I we could dig it over, turn all the soil.

June
If I do a little weeding every day it'll be clear enough.

Eric
The soil needs air, a clean start.

June
There's always going to be weeds Eric.
It's not all weeds.

Eric
They may not be weeds to you June, you know the names
but to me they're just weeds,
that is, apart from the cultivated plants.
But if it's what you want we'll do it your way.
Obviously we ought to keep the pear trees.

June
There's more than that, some shrubs and perennials too.

Eric
I was thinking it might be worth moving some things from the
garden at Salmon Pool Lane.

June
It would be good to bring plants with us.

Eric
We should go and have a look to see what the garden's doing
there.

June
I don't see why others should have what's left in our garden.

Eric
Let's go over at the weekend.
Next year this place could be something.

June
I'd love that.

Eric
We've managed to get more done now that I'm out less
evenings.

June
So much has happened since she died.
I can still see the buildings you know.
I walk down South Street
and though there's nothing on either side,

I can still see them there on either side.
I can't even remember Francis taking his exams.

Eric
There are envelopes out there I see for both of them.

June
Both at once.

Eric
That's good.

June
It'll put an end to the waiting.
I shall be glad to see the back of Peter.
Having a boy like that around all the time,
it can't have been a good influence on Francis.

Eric
Didn't they tell you?

June
What?

Eric
Francis fell into one of the ricks this week,
nearly suffocated before Peter pulled him out.
Stupid boy.

June
Peter was there first, no doubt.
I never took to him like you did.
There was little good in him coming here,
I can't imagine it's been any safer than London.

Eric
The raids stopped in May but they're still bombing London.

June
I expected a little child not a great big boy.

Eric
You would have got your results by now too.

June
If I'd kept on with it.

Eric
You made the right decision there.

June
Did I?

Eric
There's been enough on hasn't there?
Be honest now, you couldn't make head nor tail of it.

June
I might have done.

Eric
But who needs it?

June
I'd liked to have persevered
because I always wondered about the Anglo-Saxon.

Eric
How?

June
What it was, I'd like to have known.

Eric
If you don't know then there's no real loss.

June
I'd like to have made sense of it.

Eric
Look at it this way June.

June
What?

Eric
There's nothing around here more Anglo-Saxon than me.

June
Well I've got you then.

Eric *kisses her on the cheek.*

Eric
Is there any tea?

June
It's here.

June *lays out two cups and saucers.*

Eric
I wish we didn't have to use those cups.

June
There aren't any others for every day.
They're your mother's.

Eric
I know.
I wish we had some proper ones we could drink out of.

June
Look at them, they're not bad, they're Victorian, that's all.

Eric
I wouldn't mind them being out on the dresser.
They'd look all right there, for show.

June
No one would see them but us.

Eric
I'd like a nice plain cup for my tea.

June
Why go on, it's only cups.

Eric
I don't fancy it June,
when I think of all the dead people that have drunk out of
these.

June
Eric, why now?
Why so fussy?

Eric
I just noticed I don't like them.

June
Just old cups.
An ugly old cup.
Look at it, Eric.
An ugly old cup.

June *holds one up to the light and drops it.*

Eric
Why did you do that?
I didn't mean you to do that.

June
Too late.
An old cup gone.

Eric *goes to pick up some pieces.*

Eric
That's nothing really now.

June
That's right,
now really nothing.

Eric
What's up with you?

June
I don't know.
I went home the wrong way yesterday,
ended up at Salmon Pool Lane.

Eric
Here's another.
Let me pour you another cup.

June
It's habitual.

Eric
What is?

June
This, us, here.
Merely habitual.
There is no reason.

Eric
This is our home now, we live here.
We have our son. Smart boy.
Passed his exams I bet.
Eighteen years. You and I.

Don't cry June.

Peter *and* **Francis** *come in holding envelopes.*

Peter
I got my results and he got his call-up!

Francis
He means I got my results and he got his call-up.

Peter
That's what I said.

Francis *looks at broken china.*

Francis
What's this?

June
Well?

Francis
I passed them all.

Eric
What will you do now then?

Peter (*to* **Francis**)
What shall we do now?

Francis
Hey let's run to the river!

They run out.

Eric
They've gone.
Remember June.

Eric *sits beside her.*

I am here.
You are here.
And the ground's beneath our feet.

June
I know only one thing.
This feeling of loss.
It's growing.

Eric *holds* **June**.

Epilogue

Peter
It will be an eventful journey,
leaving it all green.
I know everything's going
but I'll remember what's growing.

Francis
There are no other colours.
Do we know what we have?
There's no use inventing new
and making sense,
if there's only loss
and making non-sense.

A Bucket of Eels

A Basket of Eels

Every doubt that sings
All the questions that we find
Everything anyone feels
Untidy experience of things
The flickers in your mind
It's all a bucket of eels.

Characters

Mrs Sparrow, *an old postmistress*
Nick, *a trainee manager*
April, *a free spirit*
Julia, *Ralph's sister*
Ralph, *Julia's brother*
Stella, *unemployed*

The action takes place on one night in a forest in Britain, before the end of this century.

A Bucket of Eels was first performed on 14 January 1994 in a production without décor at the Buzz Goodbody Studio, RSC, The Other Place, Stratford-upon-Avon, with the following cast:

Mrs Sparrow	Ali Troughton
Nick	Simon Coury
April	Sian Radinger
Julia	Caroline Payne
Ralph	Stephen Simms
Stella	Helen Franklin

Directed by Claire Nielson

First London Performance (in an edited version) in the Cottesloe Theatre, Royal National Theatre, on July 1st, 1995 as part of the BT Connections Festival, peformed by students of Shelley High School, Huddersfield, directed by Steven Downs.

Setting

The most convincing recreation of a wood possible on stage:
beech trees, undergrowth, bracken, brambles and nettles.
Real turf and leaves. The fragrance of damp turf and
leaf-mould brought into the theatre.

The play is set in a clearing, at least three entrances are
necessary also the facility to jump from a tree.

The firework 'A Mine of Serpents' in Act 4 shoots wriggling
snakes of light into the air, it is manufactured by Standard
Fireworks Ltd., Huddersfield, West Yorks.

Act One

In the woods, dusk. **Mrs Sparrow** *and* **Nick** *talking.* **Nick** *wears a cheap suit.*

Mrs Sparrow
An undeserved present is the best.
Like this summer;
I've not worked for it.

Nick
But it's been terrible, a bad summer.

Mrs Sparrow
Today was warm.

Nick
Was that it, the summer then, one day?
Some present.

Mrs Sparrow
It was a welcome present, today.

Nick
I've worked for it you know.
Just today; one day: it's not enough.
We deserve a better present than this.

Mrs Sparrow
I'm not talking about what we deserve, but what we get.

Nick
The woods have grown so thick,
I'd like to lie down in the leaves and die.

Mrs Sparrow
And spoil your lovely suit?
Besides it could be better tomorrow.

Nick
I don't mind. I wouldn't know if I wasn't here.

Mrs Sparrow
Yes, but if you were, you'd be glad not to have missed it.

Nick
You're right. I had hoped for good weather tomorrow.

Mrs Sparrow
You get married tomorrow.

Nick
I was going to get married tomorrow.

Mrs Sparrow
You were?

Nick
I was.

Mrs Sparrow
You was?

Nick
I'm not now, not at all.

Mrs Sparrow
Oh.

Nick
And all the presents . . .

Mrs Sparrow
. . . undeserved.

Nick
It's lucky I met you, the Postmistress.

Mrs Sparrow
I often come out here for a couple of hours.
I watch the cars on the road.

Nick
Do you think you could take a note?
It needs to get there tomorrow.

He gives her the note.

This explains that I've left and won't be back.
I'm going to spend the night to think
and in the morning I'll be gone.

Mrs Sparrow
You will wait until tomorrow, won't you?

Nick
Why?

Mrs Sparrow
Because anything could happen on the shortest night.

Nick
Before the longest day . . .

Mrs Sparrow
You're very certain.

Nick
I made up my mind.

Mrs Sparrow
What lovely writing you have.

Nick
My fountain pen. God I thought I lost it today,
I was really upset, till I found it again.

Mrs Sparrow
Nick. That's your name, isn't it?

Nick
There's no postcode on it, I'm afraid.
Perhaps you know the postcode?

Mrs Sparrow
There aren't any postcodes round here.

Nick
That's good. I like that. See you later, perhaps.

He goes.

Mrs Sparrow (*aside*)
No postcode?
No stamp!
Why should I do this?
I didn't think.
A lovelorn wood wanderer.

Enter **April**. *She has a stick.*

Mrs Sparrow
Hello.

April
Do you believe in magic?

Mrs Sparrow
When I shut my front door this evening
all the street lamps went on.

April
Often I wake up just seconds before my alarm clock goes off.

Mrs Sparrow
But I do that. It's not magic.

April
Not magic, but all magic is.

Mrs Sparrow
This magic it's not so special is it?

April
I'm not going to use an alarm clock any more.

Mrs Sparrow
Rise with the sun?

April
I want to wake up in the morning on my own.

Mrs Sparrow
I've been doing it for years, and got into the habit.
Since the clock stopped in the Post Office
I simply get on with everything.

I find more happens now.

April
Do you grow your own food too?

Mrs Sparrow
I don't have need of anything.

April
Self-sufficient then?

Mrs Sparrow
No, I have many friends.

April
I have these four-leafed clovers.

Mrs Sparrow
Are you expecting something to happen?

April
Anything.

Mrs Sparrow
And the stick?

April
That's something else.

Mrs Sparrow
Are you lost?

April
I'm glad you've talked to me.
It's what I like about it here:
people are not strangers to each other.

Mrs Sparrow
But I don't know you!

Enter **Julia**. *She holds up an apple.*

Julia
Look what someone gave me?

April
An apple.

Julia
My best wedding present.

Mrs Sparrow
Then I should eat it if I were you.

Julia
It's far too nice to eat.
But what else can a woman do with an apple?

April
You could plant it somewhere.

Mrs Sparrow
Julia this is. . . ?

April
April.

Julia
I'll call my first child April!

April
Why not May or June?

Mrs Sparrow
If it is a boy you can call him Augustus.

April
Gus!

Julia
It's all right.
I plan to have lots of children.

April
I plan to search further.
Take advantage of the light.

Mrs Sparrow
Good luck.

April *goes*.

Mrs Sparrow
So it's your big day tomorrow?

Julia
I loved everyone today.
I fell in love with the people on the bus.
I took a glance up the High Street,
and I saw everyone,
purposeful with shopping
and loved them too.

Mrs Sparrow
I know the feeling.

Julia
I could forgive anyone tonight, I see there's no malice,
because I know what people want:
And it's just love and care, that's all.

Mrs Sparrow
Tell me about the wedding, is it all planned?

Julia
We start with the cake
and there are fireworks for afterwards.

Mrs Sparrow
Do you trust him? Nick.

Julia
You have to love people unconditionally.
Trust them even to let you down occasionally.
Tomorrow, I've dreamed of it for months.
Tonight, it's as if I could embrace the air itself.

Mrs Sparrow
I remember when you couldn't come out into these woods,
not for stepping on them.

Julia
I wish my brother would come back.

Mrs Sparrow
Ralph, is he not coming for tomorrow?

Julia
It's a long training course, and very strict.

Mrs Sparrow
I can't remember where he is.

Julia
Too far to travel for one day.

Mrs Sparrow
And Nick?

Julia
Out on his stag night.

Mrs Sparrow
It's years since there's been one here.

Julia
I thought I heard something in the bracken.
You've not seen anything.

Mrs Sparrow
It's the visitor season.
I watch them, items get stolen from the Post Office.

Julia
I wonder what it was I heard.

Ralph *jumps naked from a tree.*

Ralph
Me Ralph, you Julia!

Julia
Ralph? Ralph!
Where have you been?
Ralph.
What have you done to yourself?
Oh Ralph, this is terrible.
Thank God, you're here.

Mrs Sparrow
Who do you think you are?

Ralph
I'm the wild man of the woods!

Mrs Sparrow
Pagan!

Mrs Sparrow *goes.*

Julia
Ralph.
Where have you been?

Ralph
I have come through a green labyrinth.

Julia
What?

Ralph
Come with me.
I'll take you to the marshes,
we'll lie there at dawn,
naked under the water,
just eyes and nostrils above the surface.
You can feel the eels brush you,
frogs climb on you:
and when the sun rises
you'll see the steam over you.

Julia
No Ralph, I can't.

Ralph
Let's go now.

Julia
What is it, this green labyrinth?

Ralph
I've been travelling, all over, hundreds of miles and mostly at night. Often I've come to cities and turned from the yellow lights. Where I can I keep to the forestry, and only cross the open land in darkness. I've kept clear of the motorways, not following any path, except twice I came to the coast, I don't know which, and then I followed the shore for a while. I couldn't tell you which counties, woods, cities or seas I've seen. I determined to lose track; perhaps I crossed my own path sometimes, even doubled up part of the journey. It has been a green labyrinth. Come now, share it with me.

Julia
I can't Ralph, I'm getting married tomorrow.
Look this apple, it's a wedding present.

He takes it.

Don't eat it.

He eats it.

Ralph
You getting married?

Julia
Yes.

He snorts.

Julia
I hate not knowing where you are.
You could have stayed at home and signed on.
Where have you been?
I write you letters in my head.

Ralph
What do you expect, replies?

Julia
We've all lied for you, you know.

Ralph
I didn't ask anyone to cover up.

Julia
Why can't you do something for me?
Couldn't you just come to the wedding?

Ralph
Like this?

Julia
You'd need a bath.

Ralph
Why this sudden marriage interest?

Julia
Six months! The longest I've not seen you.
Everyone has to make their way in the world.
I'm twenty-nine, in less than twelve years I'll be over forty.

Ralph
Is he performing the service?
Our father in heaven.

Julia
Yes he is. They've been worried you know.
She blames him and they're not talking.
Can't you see why I want you there?
You've not even met my husband.

Ralph
What's he like?

Julia
Different.

Ralph
He'll need to be. Does he know anything about me?

Julia
No, nothing, what could I say?

Ralph
Would I like him?

Julia
He and you are the most important people to me now,
that's why I want you to meet.

Ralph
He and I, eh? He, and I.
Come with me Julia.

Julia
Stop it Ralph, let go of me.
Don't look at me.

I've thought of you for months, missed you!
but at this moment I wish you'd not come back.
It's as if you weren't my brother at all, it means nothing.

Ralph
I'll be off then.

Julia
Don't do that.

Ralph
Goodbye whoever you are,
have a happy marriage.

Julia
I don't understand, we've not talked yet.

Ralph
We've talked enough.

Julia
What do you eat?

Ralph
I take vegetables from the fields and I killed some sheep.
Cut them up with my knife.

Julia
What are you up to? When shall I see you?

Ralph
You won't, unless you come now.

Julia
Don't say that.

Ralph
You and I, we're tied, a blood tie, the only real tie.

He kisses her.

Julia
I do want to be with you.

Ralph
You have a choice.

Julia
You're giving me a choice?
I can't do what you do.
I don't want to escape, run away.

Ralph
I've never spent so many months on my own, it's no escape.

Julia
Tomorrow, that's really important to me.

Ralph
Brother or husband?
Husband or brother?

Julia
Doesn't it look as if I've chosen,
I shall go to my wedding tomorrow,
I'll be his wife, but still your sister.
It's not a choice.

Ralph
Except now.

He makes to go.

This is the end.

Julia
No!

Ralph (*he holds out his hand*)
This is the beginning?

Julia
No!

Ralph
What then?

Julia
Just part-way.

She runs off, he sits.

Nick *enters.*

Nick
Did I hear a voice?

Ralph
There was a woman here.

Nick
Oh I know who that was.

Ralph
Who are you?

Nick
Just a visitor.

Ralph
Where are you going?

Nick
I haven't decided.
Do you live here?

Ralph
No.

Nick
Me neither.
Where do you stay?

Ralph
I just lie down in the leaves at night.

Nick
That's what I'm always saying.
What do you do?

Ralph
Each night's supper provides every day's occupation.

Nick
Like everyone else.

Ralph
Can you take care of yourself?

Nick
Yes.

Ralph
Then do it, and try not to hurt anyone else.

Nick
I get these attacks of why?

Ralph
Why?

Nick
Yes.

Ralph
There's only doing and getting, keeping on.

Nick
Do you have a sense of humour?

Ralph
Hah! That was below the belt.

Nick
It's not a question with an answer?

Ralph
Why did I start talking to you?
No chat for months and now this.

Nick
It's an attractive game, running naked on a summer's night,
but in winter?

Ralph
I'll roll in the snow to warm my flesh
and by then my feet will be hardened sufficiently.

Nick
I don't believe you.
Why not make a fire?
Or build a house?

Ralph
You live with the cold.

Nick
And if it's like last year?

Ralph
Then you be careful not to stand on a rock
or it takes the skin off your foot.

Nick
You're disturbed, upset.

Ralph
I'm not a case.

Nick
Perhaps you act more strangely than you realise.

Ralph
Everyone's more self-deceiving than they know.

Nick
Can I come with you?

Ralph
This'd not be comfortable.

Nick
It must be killing you.

Ralph
I get to look at things as they are.

Nick
Do you think we are social creatures?

Ralph
Isn't it what sets us above the apes?
Collaboration.

Nick
Perhaps we made a mistake?
Contradictions abound!
First there's our relatives, we rarely get on with them.
As soon as we are old enough, we escape.

Secondly, we expect to choose others to live with and get on
with better than the relatives we had to live with.

And the result is spending your life doing what you don't
like, for reasons you don't comprehend.

Couples; it doesn't work.
Coupling; it doesn't interest me.

Ralph
So why do people do it?
Even my sister's getting married.

Nick
People feel incomplete.
No one wants to take care of themselves;
so they make a bargain:
you take care of me, I'll take care of you.
Taking care of you, I'm taking care of me;
and it becomes: my wife before you, my husband before you
and our children before everyone.
Horrible!

Ralph
But natural.

Nick
It doesn't make for a generous world.

Ralph
You expect a generous world?

Nick
I don't know.
But to do what you do, I see that as the best challenge.

Ralph *kisses* **Nick**. *He takes* **Ralph**'s *hand*.

Ralph
Into the night then.

Exit **Ralph** *and* **Nick**.

Enter **Julia** *from elsewhere*.

Julia
Ralph?

(*Aside*.) Gone.

Act Two

Late. **Julia** *and* **Mrs Sparrow** *talking.*

Julia
I had a bath.
I didn't recognise my body in the bath.
I knew something was going to happen.
I made tea. I poured tea into the milk jug.
I knew it would be like this.

Mrs Sparrow
Tomorrow, it will be all right.

Julia
Why should I let Ralph spoil my day?

Mrs Sparrow
Nothing will happen after all.

Julia
He wasn't going to come,
and now he isn't going to come.

Mrs Sparrow
Exactly. What's the difference?

Julia
My father will regret he ever let him go outward bound.

Mrs Sparrow
Your brother, he always was an outdoor man.

Julia
He misses Ralph.
He says he feels outnumbered, by women, two to one.
He puts the lavatory seat up. We put it down.
He says he's losing grip.

Mrs Sparrow
So Ralph's return would even things up?

Julia
No, my departure will do that.

Mrs Sparrow
Unless Stella finds him.

Julia
I don't hold out much hope.

Mrs Sparrow
Never dismiss the kindness of strangers, even tourists.

Julia
I went to Ralph's old room, earlier.
Nick stays there tonight.
I sat at the window, curtains open
and found I was waiting, hoping he'd come.

Mrs Sparrow
Why did you come out?

Julia
I felt alone and I got to thinking.
I didn't want to go to my single bed again.
I wanted the night to be over.

Mrs Sparrow
Will you sleep now?

Julia
I'd like to find Nick. Wake him, should I?
Does that shock you?

Mrs Sparrow
I understand.

Julia
I'd rather not be understood, no mystery then.

Mrs Sparrow
You lied to me earlier, about Ralph.

Julia
That wasn't a lie, it was a secret.

Mrs Sparrow
Is there a distinction?

Julia
Should I tell him?
Nick.

He has to know one day.
It's an uncomfortable secret.

Mrs Sparrow
Not tonight. Let it wait.

Julia
I am so incredibly angry what can I do?

Mrs Sparrow
Are you warm enough?

Julia
Quite warm enough, but tired.
I must make an effort to be my best.

Mrs Sparrow
Let me take you back.

They go.

Enter **Nick** *and* **Stella** *from opposite directions.* **Nick** *is dirty and has lost his jacket and tie.*

Stella
Julia sent me.

Nick
Ah!

Stella
You know who that is?

Nick
Yes.

Stella
Then you're the man I'm looking for.
She sent me to look for you.

Nick
What?

Stella
Now then: she wants you to come back for tomorrow.
She wants you to understand that even after the wedding there's no reason why you can't communicate. She says that she isn't at all ashamed of you and she asked me to emphasise that it's very important to her that you be there.

Nick (*aside*)
My head it's a gyroscope!

Stella
I just met her and I'm only doing this as a favour because she is so upset, but I think she will go ahead without you if necessary.

Nick
How?

Stella
What's happened to you?

Nick
I met this man in the woods, he was strange, he didn't have any shoes on; but he's gone now. He took me all over the place, and though we walked for hours, perhaps he led me in a circle, because I think I was here before.

Stella
Déjà vu perhaps?

Nick (*aside*)
Just when I decided to go back,
get the note back, now it's too late!

Stella
She cried.

Nick (*aside*)
And when you want a letter to get there it never does . . .

Stella
She was frantic.

Nick
Thank God I met you.

(*Aside.*) It's better to know . . .

Stella
She sat and brushed her lips on the back of her hand.

Nick (*aside*)
What if I had turned up after the note?
Horrible!

Stella
Only a madman would be out in these woods at night:
I've done my bit, goodbye.

Nick
Hey! Where are you off to? Can I come with you?

Ralph *enters with a lump of cake.*

Stella
Another one!

Ralph
Who wants cake?

Stella
Christmas cake in summer?

Ralph
Wedding cake!

Stella
Who's getting married?

Nick
Not me!

Stella
You stole this?

Ralph
Yes.

Nick (*aside*)
All my life is slipping away tonight . . .

Ralph
Look at the sky, it's like an aquarium or a deep swimming pool, upside down.
And filled with stars.

Nick (*aside*)
I was on the brink and now I'm falling.

Stella
You don't think what you see is what's there do you?
How nostalgic can you get!

Nick
Everything slips through my hands . . .

Stella
So you're the strange man with no shoes on.
He told me.

Ralph
He asked to come with me.

Stella
He asked me that too.

Ralph *threatens* **Nick** *with his knife.*

Ralph
I could kill you and you wouldn't know it.

Nick (*to* **Ralph**)
You have such brown eyes.

Ralph (*to* **Nick**)
Cut your wrists with a blade of grass?

Stella
Is it possible?

Ralph
A reed would be easier.

Nick
I'm snatching at water!

Ralph
It's warmer at night. You can slip beneath the surface,
lean back, lie back, let yourself down into the black water.
Would you like that?

Stella
It's not dark here is it?
I've been walking in the half light.
I expected pitch darkness.

Ralph
It's only the lights over there that make it feel dark out here.

Nick
I don't agree! It's dark here.
I've never been anywhere so fucking black!

Ralph *slaps him.*

Stella
What's wrong with him?

Ralph
He's feeling incomplete.

Nick
The grass it's heaving,
as if the soil were breathing.

Stella
You never know what you might step on out here.

Ralph
With bare feet you know where you step.

Ralph *wrestles* **Nick**'s *shoes and socks from him.*

Nick
Why are you doing this to me?

Ralph
It only takes two months for the skin to harden.

Nick
How will I manage without my shoes?

Ralph
People managed before.

Nick
No. No. No!

Stella *assists* **Ralph** *in restraining* **Nick**.

Stella
Do you know him?

Ralph
No. Do you know him?

Stella
No.

Ralph
All strangers then.

Nick
My stomach it's churning.
Eels at the root of my gut!

Stella
Would cake cheer him up?

Nick
I'll not eat what's been on the ground.

Ralph
Everything's been on the ground.

Stella
He should eat some of that cake.

They struggle to force cake into **Nick***'s mouth.*

Nick
I'll not stomach this.

He goes.

Ralph
Do you want cake?

Stella
I don't like it.
Perhaps we could have been more sympathetic?

Ralph
He got what he deserved.

She looks. A point of light crosses the sky.

Stella
A shooting star.

Ralph
We know that was there.

Stella
It was there; or it was a plane.

Ralph
What about the moon?
We've been there, know about that.

Stella
The event of our lives; and it's forgotten.

Ralph
Dates have become titles for science fiction.

Time has been parcelled out.
The decades are so distinct,
I can't fit this century together.

Stella
We are the fools;
fools confined in a corner,
the scuffed corner of history,
a dog-ear of time.

Ralph
Such a monumental labour
to carve out the world
and we've left a great big hollow
with a little hard egg.

Stella
How long have we got?

Ralph
They may have lost thirty-two years somewhere,
and eleven days somewhere else,
but it's nearly done.
A crack between the clock's hands' clap! (*He claps.*)

Stella
Everyone thinks they're getting somewhere
and they're not.
I watch people running in the park
and I wonder, what are they running from?

Ralph
Perhaps they are only running?

Stella
Have you been Inside?

Ralph
No; outside for six months.

Stella
Do you have a Disease or something?

Ralph
No. I just eat irregularly.

Stella
Are you living on the dole too then?

Ralph
On my six wits.

Stella
If the world doesn't owe us a living
what do we owe the world?

Ralph
Why should we do anything?
It's late at night.
I like just to be somewhere like this.

Stella
How did you take to the wild life?

Ralph
I was here once.
Trees overwhelmed me.
I walked beneath them.
I went up to one, wrapped myself against it,
clasped the trunk in a great hug, gripped it between my legs,
the bark on my face.
Inside me, I had changes.
From then on, I came back often,
and walked here for miles,
naked at night.
So it became the only choice,
when events turned out as they did.

Stella
It must be odd out here,
quite different from getting undressed in a room.

Ralph
You put your clothes on a branch and walk away . . .

Stella
Don't ever try this in a park will you?
or you'll get arrested.

Ralph
What happened to you?

Stella
What do you do when you don't want to go home?
I walked on.

Ralph
Didn't you have friends?

Stella
You think you know someone and you don't.
You don't know anyone.
However many friends you have, it doesn't matter.

Ralph
But we hit it off instantly!

Stella
I don't have a scrap of self-pity.
I wouldn't have done this if it didn't thrill me.
It has been my most vivid year.
The most taste, the most smell, the most colours I've seen.

Ralph
Do you cry often?

Stella
No one talks you know.
People sit on transport,
faces knotted and don't speak.
I started a one-woman campaign:
spoke simply to provoke.
You should see how annoyed they get.

Ralph
But I like not-talking.

Stella
I want just to communicate.
They think you're after something.
It's the healthy ones interest me.
You especially.

Ralph
Me, healthy?

Stella
You are the most alive one I've met.

Ralph
Natural man meets strange woman!

Stella
For me it's been back to the wall
and for you it's been back to the woods.

Ralph
Let's not talk much now,
or we'll get bored with each other too quickly.
I like blackcurrants at night; after cake.
Shall we get some?

Stella
The world's out there.

Ralph
Believe me there's a world here.

Stella
Most of humanity I despise them.

Ralph
Me too!

Stella
Isn't it lucky I like you?

Ralph
It wasn't luck.

Stella
What else leads us where we go?

Ralph
Blackcurrants?

Stella
Let's go together then.

They go.

Nick *returns searching.*

Nick
They must be here somewhere.

April *enters.*

April
I am a tiger.

Nick
Where are my shoes?

April
Let's fight like tigers!

Nick
I'm looking for my shoes.

April
Leave it. Don't tell me. I like it:
the Unexplained.
Perhaps you walk on hot coals?

Nick
My life it only seems like that.

April
Aren't you going to ask about me?

Nick
No. I don't care.
Not out for a walk, that's certain.
People never are, there's always more to it than that.

April
It's true. I've come for the light.

Nick
Then you've come to the wrong place.

April
The light at dawn, at midsummer.
All sorts of things can be revealed.

Nick
I'm looking for a friend, a little bit of quiet and a true friend.

(*Aside.*) Why did he go off?

April
You can come with me.

Nick
No thanks.

April
Accept it then, there's no one else here.
You alone.

Nick
It's not true.
This place it's crawling with people.
Where I am,
I don't know if I should be here.
What I am doing,
I'm not sure if I should be doing it.
Perhaps I need a sign?

April
Fate, I believe in that.
Nothing is as random as you think.

Nick
Perhaps it's my destiny to be like this?

April
No. Unhappiness it's a vice.

Nick
I have such bad luck with people.

April
Everyone gets an even deal of luck.

Nick
How's that?

April
It's the inequality of chance.
A coin is as likely to fall heads as tails.
Yet after five hundred times heads,
it is no less likely to be tails next time.

Nick
Explain it.

April
You need to think of your own example.

Nick
Hmm! Can't think of any now.
I have to admit I am confused.

April
That's a good start.

Nick
Sometimes I wake in the night
I hear someone call my name;
and I half recognise the voice,
but I don't know who it is.

April
The Unexplained, we have to look at it rationally.
I can see you appreciate what I'm talking about.
Look at you, you're very untidy.

Nick
But this is just how I am tonight; you are too.

April
It's how things are.

Nick
What things?

April
These are the twin principles: the Untidy and the Unexplained.

Nick
It's a mystery to me.

April
You've got the picture.
Believe me, all over the world
people are thinking like this.
It's exciting isn't it?
Such a lot we'll never know.
Whole new fields opening up.

Nick
Fields with cows in them, that's all I know about.

April
Yes, but how do you know they're there?

Nick
Because the milk comes every morning.

April
It's a new era.
Doesn't it thrill you?

Nick
You are the most inconsistent person I've ever met.

April
I'm talking about a lot of old knowledge, dug up.

Nick
A lot of old ignorance you mean.
I may be blind but I'm walking in the dark.
I don't know where I'll get to, but I'm going.

He goes.

April (*aside*)
At least I know I'm lost.

She lies down in the leaves, clutching the stick.

I want to be covered.
I want to be pressed into the ground;
and I want to know nothing.

Julia *enters.*

Julia
Nick?
I'm looking for a husband.

April
You were the woman who wanted children.

Julia
Yes.

April
There was a man here with no shoes on.

Julia
Him. What did he say?

April
He was unhappy. He was looking for a friend.

Julia
Poor Ralph. Completely alone.
I shouldn't have left him.

April
It was someone particular, but not you.
He said it was a he.

Julia (*aside*)
Strange.

(*To* **April**.)
If you meet him again tell him I forgive him completely.
Say I beg him to come back.
I'll stick with him for life now.
How I wish Nick was here, he'd find Ralph.
How I need him now.
And to think I was full of guilt,
because of my impatience and anger.

April
Guilt it's not an admirable emotion.
But your impatience and anger,
they are virtues.

Julia
Where can Nick be?
I had a secret to tell him; it's a problem.
I'm frightened. What shall I do?

April
A secret is something you choose not to say.
But what about the things you don't know,
that you can't choose to say?

Julia
It's the things you don't know you know that frighten me.
You still have the stick, I see.

April
Every woman should carry a stick.
You never know what you might find.

Julia
First my brother ran away,
then my husband went missing
now I can't even find my father.
What's happened to all the men?
Why is everything suddenly in such chaos?
or is it my imagination?

April
It always has been
and now you've come to see it.

Julia
All these disasters,
storms, fires, crises,
sometimes I think I did them,
I hear the news and I think 'What have I done?'
That's stupid isn't it?

April
No. What fascinate me are the things
you don't know you don't know.

Julia
Oh, life's too short to worry about them.

April
Exactly.

Julia
So what's the answer?

April
They are all inside you anyway!

Julia
As I suspected, my fears are rootless.
I'll take one last look round and go home.

She goes.

April (*aside*)
It's too easy to dismiss what you can't explain.

Act Three

Early. **Mrs Sparrow** *and* **April** *talking.* **Mrs Sparrow** *has the note.*

Mrs Sparrow
There are two kinds of people in this world.
Those who go to the lavatory and those that don't.
That's my opinion.

April
Not everyone admits what they can do.

Mrs Sparrow
Mostly I'm concerned with the things I didn't do.

April
But you've obviously achieved such a lot:
the Post Office.
Think of all those millions of letters delivered.

Mrs Sparrow
Have you seen Julia?

April
She was looking for that man, the one with no shoes on.
She gave me a message. She said I was to say she begged
him to come back and to tell him she'd stick with him for life
if he did.

Mrs Sparrow
A family reconciliation might help things.

April
She said she wanted children.
She wants to marry him.

Mrs Sparrow
Who's this? Who? Did she mention his name?

April
Ralph, that's what she called him. I'm certain of it.

Mrs Sparrow
There are some things you'd rather not know aren't there?

April
Why need she marry him, just to have children?

Mrs Sparrow
Marriage, that's an obscene idea!

April
It's not for everyone.

Mrs Sparrow
Perhaps I should go now and tell the parents?

April
Why do people blame parents when it comes to sex?

Ralph and **Stella** *enter, heavily smeared with blackcurrant juice.*

Ralph
Because no one can imagine their parents doing it.

Mrs Sparrow
Where did you come from?

Ralph
I was under a blackcurrant bush.

Stella
That's a lie.

Ralph
Everyone doesn't speak truth.

Stella
That's a lie too.

Mrs Sparrow
I'd prefer it if it was so.

Stella
I found him.

Mrs Sparrow
I wish you'd not tried.
I wish you'd go away and not come back.

Stella
You're the ungrateful one.
Why is it people like you
always treat people like us,

like this?
No wonder he ran away.

April
Why this conflict,
is it the temperature?

Mrs Sparrow
I must say what I think.
This animal instinct,
you need to curb it.

Mrs Sparrow *goes*.

April
Are you a savage beast then?

Ralph
Everyone likes a good quarrel.

Stella
You have to recognise injustice.

April
There's no injustice.
All's for us to learn from.

Stella
And the holocaust, bombs, cancer?
They're not bad?

April
You don't understand.

Stella (*to* **Ralph**)
Why did she turn on me?

Ralph
Is it my fault?

April
Everything that happens you choose it.

Stella
What did I do wrong?

April
You create your own world entirely.

Ralph
Our parents, did we choose them?

Stella
Perhaps you'll learn something from this?

Stella *breaks* **April**'s *stick*.

April
I reject your violence
because I have no doubt you have a right to feel alienated.

Ralph
Can't you allow us a bit of fun?
It's just an old stick.

April
I use it to find things beneath the soil.
There's always water moving underground.
I can feel it.

Stella
What nonsense!
How can you feel a thing like that?
I went to the biggest cemetery there is.
A hundred and eighty thousand dead,
beneath my feet,
and I felt nothing.

Ralph
Isn't there a machine you can get to do that,
detect things underground?

April
There's always a ghost in the device,
any machine inherits the quality of its maker.

Stella
Last time I bought a ticket
the machine spat it out.
The thing hit me in the chest
and fell on the floor.

Ralph
We used to have a microwave
until I put a hot water bottle in it.
Nothing works properly.

April
Back to nature,
is that the answer?
I'm attracted too.

Ralph
What exactly are you searching for tonight?

April
A man.

Stella
I've heard this before.

Ralph
I'm a man, perhaps it was me you wanted?

April
The one who was unhappy,
have you seen him?
Julia gave me a message.
She begs him to come back.
Do you know who that is?

Stella
You too.

Ralph
It all joins up now!

April
How much do you embrace?

Ralph
Everything! It's tangled up.

April
At last! What I've been searching for.

Stella
What's going on?

Ralph
This is chaos:
EVERYTHING'S ALL MIXED UP!

April
You have said it.

The pulse of nature,
I have felt it.
Now I go.
Thank you.

April *goes.*

Ralph
I think I begin to understand something.

Ralph *picks up the stick.*

Ugh!

Stella
What is it?

He throws it into the bushes.

Ralph
It twitched!
The stick twitched.

Stella
Are you all right?

Ralph
This is just life coursing through my veins,
but I don't know what that was.

Stella
The imagination can play tricks.

Ralph
Questions breed.

Stella
Where do questions get you?

Ralph
Sometimes I'm far from anywhere.

Stella
This life's untenable.
One day they'll find you
in a marsh somewhere

half-starved and dead of exposure.
Doesn't that frighten you?

Ralph
No.
What frightens me
is when a branch lashes unexpectedly
and you think there's something there.

Stella
What kind of thing?

Ralph
You know what I mean,
everyone's minds are similar in this respect:
A scaly pig-wolf thing
with serrated teeth and big claws.
It doesn't matter how educated you are,
it's still there crouching
horns pricked, eyes a-glitter, and wheezing smoke.

Stella
You are a curious lad.
Is that why you stay awake at night?
It's not the things of any other world that frighten me
but what people can do in this.
Just walking out here reminds me
of those bodies they find in the woods,
so decayed they have to remake the faces
even to guess who they were.
That's years ago now,
but I still can't go to the dentist
without feeling it's my face he's remodelling in clay
onto the skull bone.
Just the touch of these leaves
and I'm being laid beneath them,
seven years old and still clutching my satchel,
warm blood on the skin.

Ralph
All the soil is dead people.
Everything you eat is dead people.
Everything you drink passed through dead people first.

It's what we're made of:
we are dead people.

Stella
You should never say a thing like that,
because you never know what could happen.

Ralph
Then let's say all the dead people are living:
I got up from under the leaves and walked.
It also follows that we are everyone.
What everyone does we do.
What shall we do?

Stella
Let's go!

Ralph
How?

Stella
Get off. Get out. Go.
Why did anyone ever come here?
It was a mistake.
A bad idea to begin with.
This climate it's inhuman.

Ralph
Not inhuman, merely indifferent.

Stella
What's the earliest date you can remember?

Ralph
1066.

Stella
Less than a thousand years.
History's not begun here yet.

Ralph
But I found some Roman coins.

Stella
Brought from elsewhere . . .
This is not the ancient world.

Ralph
What about the early people who walked across the marshes
of the North Sea?

Stella
They began their journey somewhere else.
It's why people can't bear immigrants like me.
They only just stopped being immigrants themselves.
What's so special about this place?
The weather is a disaster.
It makes everyone miserable.

Ralph
Today was good. I lay in the sun for hours.

Stella
It's a big enough world.
Why spend your life in one corner?

Ralph
How do we travel over the water?
Now the Channel's not a marsh.

Stella
When I was eleven,
I climbed a runway fence,
got on a plane, ended up in Madrid.

Ralph
My sister has some plane tickets,
we could get them.

The branches lash, **Nick** *emerges, his clothes torn.*

Nick
Ralph, at last I've found you again!

Stella
Your feet, they're bleeding!
Don't cry.
Nick, your life is it all right?

Nick
I could cut up a sheep!
I can learn to swim!
You said you stole.

I do it too, in shops.
Only small things
but you should see how excited I get.

Ralph
You rub your face in the dirt don't you?

Nick
I'm a man of the soil now.
Ralph.
Please listen.
It means the earth.
Let me join you.

Ralph
You wouldn't last a minute out here.

Nick
It doesn't matter what you say.
I still want to do what you do.
My skin will harden too!

Nick *flings his shirt away. He begins to tear his trousers off.* **Ralph**
and **Stella** *go to stop him. They all grapple together.*

Stella (*to* **Nick**)
I saw him first!

Ralph
That's not so.

Julia *enters.*

Julia
You. You. And You!

Nick
Ah! Ah! Ah!

Julia
I went back and you weren't there.
I came out and you're back.
And you here, with them!

Ralph
He's with me.

Stella
I found him.

Nick
Hello.

Ralph
Do you two know each other?

Julia
He's my husband.

Stella
She's his brother.

Nick *and* **Ralph**
What?

Nick
Do you two know each other?

Ralph She's my sister. }
Julia He's my brother. }

Stella
What?

Nick
What?

Julia (*to* **Nick**)
What are you doing here?
You'd better wash your feet in the bath when we get home.

Stella }
Ralph } He asked to come with me.

Ralph
You two do know each other!

Julia
Who do you think you are?

Ralph
A free man.

Julia
An outlaw!
What would happen if everyone thought like this?
Someone has to work.

Ralph
Don't work!
Millions can't be wrong.

Julia
Too many don't work, and they didn't choose.
The world doesn't run on its own.
Someone has to keep it going.
What gives you the right to behave like this?
Take what belongs to others?

Ralph
Not everything belongs to someone.

Julia
You are so green!
Everything I have, I have because I worked for it.
You have to work to achieve anything.

Ralph
Why work?

Julia
It's all we have to do. Most of us work to live.
We try to give our best in the service of others.

Ralph
Why should others want what you have to give?

Julia
I'd rather work than be unemployed.

Ralph
Then that's just vanity, and fear.

Julia
Fear and vanity?

She hits him.

Ralph
Yes.

Julia
What about self-esteem?

She licks her hand.

Blackcurrants!
All over your face.
There are no blackcurrants yet?
You've been home.
What have you done?
Don't you care about your mother and father?

Ralph
They are here.

Julia
No they're not, they're over there.

Ralph
They are in us.
We are them.
They are us. We are here.
I care, but I don't need to see them.

Julia
You are a selfish man.

Ralph
I am you.
You are me.
Meet you,
meeting me.

Julia
Don't make me think now.

(*Aside.*) I wanted to go to bed early.
I look forward to that, the moment I switch off.

Ralph
Listen to me. I am your redundant brother.

Julia
I'm not like you, Ralph.
I'm strange.
When it's raining I want to go indoors.
I like to read letters in the morning,
wash sweaters in the afternoon,
and cook supper in the evening.
When it's wet I prefer to be dry.
When it's cold I prefer to be warm.

None of this is as remarkable as you think.
It's what civilisation means.

Nick, shall we go home now?

Nick
No.

Julia
Why not?

Nick
I cannot do it.
I cannot give you that look.
You want a look of love.
I cannot give it.
I do not think I love you any more.

(And who's that?)

Julia
What about me?
I have it here.

Nick
If anyone is,
I am not for you.
Didn't you hear what I've been telling you?
(And why didn't you tell me about him?)
What did you expect?

Julia
Not this. Why now? Why not today?
What about tomorrow?

Nick
Today: it wasn't possible.
Tonight: it turned out this way.
and now Tomorrow: it won't happen.

Julia
You were the only person I ever chose.
You loved me?

Nick
I loved you.
I try to love you.

Julia
I don't want that. I want to be held by you.

Nick
I wish I could have loved you a bit longer.
(I wish you'd told me about him.)

Julia
The love of my life.
I had hopes.
You and I we could have had something.

Nick
We had it.
Don't be disappointed.

Julia
All my hopes have been destroyed,
how can I be disappointed?

Nick
You meet people once.
You love people once.
You lose people once.
So the next person you meet,
look them in the eye.

Julia
I want to get along.
Just let me get along.

Ralph
Here is a chance.

Julia
He took his chance.

Ralph
You have a chance.

Julia
He took my chance.

Ralph
We all have a chance,
but no one wants to look,
no one wants to think.

Julia
I prefer not to think.
I don't deserve this.

Ralph
You only have one chance.
And there you go, there you go,
throw away your only chance!

Julia
Was it you? or you?
What did you do to him?

Stella
You're not going to marry your brother are you?

Julia (*to* **Ralph**)
Did you take your chance with him?

Nick
It's no one's fault.

Julia
Everything in this world is someone's fault.

Nick
Don't take the responsibility on yourself.

Julia
It's not me I blame.

Nick
We have to tolerate each other,
we are all tolerated to some degree.

Julia
Ralph. How I dislike you.
I do not love you any more.
I hate you.
I could kill you.
Kill you and be quite happy.

Ralph
Except you haven't got it in you.

Julia
I could get your father's rabbit gun and shoot you down.

Stella
How can you say that to anyone?

Julia
He's my brother.
I can say what I like to him.
I'm allowed to hate him,
if I want to.

Ralph
We used to say that to each other when we were small.

Julia
I can see you have got together,
and it's been a plot,
a filthy plot.
It seems to me there's nothing left to say.

Stella
Take care of yourself.

Exit **Julia**.

Nick (*aside*)
She deceived me!
Why am I still here?
Why did I not go?
Hope can be a bad master.

Nick *retrieves his shirt.*

Stella
Did you love her?

Nick
I think I did.

Stella
If you love someone, you know it.
And if you don't, you don't.
She does.

Nick
I've been walking around with tears in my eyes for a month,
and she didn't notice, she was dreaming I think,
stars in hers.

Ralph
She had a lucky escape from you.

Nick
Thanks Ralph, can I have my shoes back now?

Ralph
I don't know where they are.
Haven't you more important things to consider?

Nick
It's not the same any more.
You've changed.

Ralph
You're a dog.

Nick
How?

Ralph
All men are dogs,
we have thighs like dogs.

Act Four

Not yet dawn. **Nick** *is urinating.* **Julia** *enters.*

Nick
Ah!

Julia
You.

Nick
I'm sorry.

Julia
I can take anything except apology.

Nick
I had to go somewhere.

Julia
Don't lick your finger.

Nick
It was wet, I didn't think.

Julia
Couldn't you have gone earlier?

Nick
I had to go now, it's how men are.

Julia
You could have gone back.

Nick
Too late.

Julia
Is it?

Nick
Julia.
If you ever need a hand, I am still your friend. Should you ever want any help I am still here, or would come if you called. If you ever wanted to come and find me, then do. If there's ever anything you need that I have, or could get for you, ask me.

As long as I am here I would support you.
I don't know why any of this is so,
except that your well-being is important to me.
And as far as I am concerned all this stands for always.

Julia
No one has ever hurt me as much as you did.
It became that I had no words
I could even share with you.
I could not speak.
Now I know that what you did is wrong,
but in spite of what you said I do not dislike you.

Nick
You loved me?

Julia
Yes.
You could not have been wholly aware of what you have done,
and so I wanted you to know that your act has had no effect
upon me, in case you should have regret.

Nick
Your face . . .

Julia
My face?

Nick
His face. I can see you have his face, it looks strange on you,
twisted and altered, and your hair it's different.
What can it be like to have a brother?

Julia
You'll never know.

Nick
Yes.

Julia
Sometimes you can drink coffee and think it tea.
Is that what happened here?

Nick
All I see now

is figures of people
before my eyes.

Julia
When you came near
I should have seen
you came by.

Nick
See you sometime then.

He kisses her.

Julia
I was askew,
but I do know what I do.

Nick *goes.*

Julia (*aside*)
He's gone,
run away,
from the wedding;
gone completely.
Who's going to cuddle me up now?
It's all I wanted
an hour ago,
and now?

Mrs Sparrow *enters.*

Julia
I never expected to be out all night.
I must look terrible.
My skin it's so flawed.
I hate it. I hate my skin.

Mrs Sparrow
You wear your doubts on your face.

Julia
Every time I look in the mirror,
it's the imperfections strike me first.

Mrs Sparrow
Better to have them on the outside,
where you can see them.

Julia
Is it?
Did you come to find me?

Mrs Sparrow
Yes.
The worst thing about this is that
you have lost solitude,
you can't bear to be alone.
But one day you will walk into an empty room and be thankful,
from then on you will be all right.

You and Ralph: let's not talk about it.
Has he gone back to the training course now?

Julia
Training, it's what they do to trees.

Mrs Sparrow
That boy needs training.

Julia
Ralph, he was born in a field with the gate open!

Mrs Sparrow
Forget about your brother. He's no good.
I am more concerned about you than him.

Julia
He is a pig.

Mrs Sparrow
A sister and a brother
shouldn't love each other.
I understand you. No mystery now.

Julia
Did you know we were twins?
Neither of us knows which is the twin.
We have been measured against each other,
measured ourselves against ourselves,
and we have both suffered.

Mrs Sparrow
Perhaps you should try to live with yourself?

Julia
How can you? When there's never you alone,
always you with the other.

Mrs Sparrow
Mostly there's just me.

Julia
Perhaps I will think differently,
when I get to your age.

Mrs Sparrow
At your age I was my age,
I think everyone always is.

Julia
I can see
I shall remember tonight
for the rest of my life.
These hours are etched in my mind.
I had this feeling earlier too, today.
Already it seems months ago,
now tonight has gone.

Mrs Sparrow
Did you sleep?

Julia
I was cold, I put the heater on,
I needed air,
I opened the window.

Mrs Sparrow
You had a little rest then?

Julia
I couldn't sleep for long
but I had a dream.
I was being force-fed eels,
a bucket of eels inside me.

Mrs Sparrow
What can have brought this on?

Julia
Do you think I shall have a child?

Mrs Sparrow
The best you can hope for is to sleep now.

Julia
I woke to find patterns in the room,
a sharp-edged print by moonlight,
squares on me.

Mrs Sparrow
So you're feeling better?

Julia
I'm not better,
I'm just acting.

Mrs Sparrow
What now?

Julia
I want a cake.
I'm going now to get a cake.

Mrs Sparrow
What for?

Julia
To eat. I must get one to eat, for my breakfast.
I'll go alone and eat my cake.
How did you know I might be here?

Mrs Sparrow
When you get to my age you know these things.

Julia
I hope I shall.

She goes.

Mrs Sparrow *takes out the letter.*

Mrs Sparrow (*aside*)
In spite of this gentle face,
I am an old square peg.
And though I may look soft
I have hard wooden corners.

Often I like myself very little
and it doesn't matter!
Sometimes it's better to say nothing.

She rips up the letter, then goes.

Nick *comes from where he has been concealed to gather the scraps of his letter.*

Nick (*aside*)
So it never got there.
That's the Post Office!
I could've gone back, but can't now.
It's too late,
and I don't want to
as I couldn't then.
What did Julia think?
Why did she say what she did?
It's a mystery – the unexplained.
Phew!
What an escape.

Ralph *and* **Stella** *enter.* **Ralph** *has a bag.*

Nick
I'm a free man now,
and I don't know what to do.

Stella
You've got a job.

Nick
A job is not what you do.

Ralph
You've got things.
Spend your money.

Nick
I've no money.
Just thirteen letters from the bank,
unopened.

Stella
Perhaps you'd like some cake now?

Nick
I'd like to try it.
See what it tastes like.

Ralph *breaks up a dirty lump of cake.*

Ralph
Brush the mud off first!

Nick
Woops.

Ralph
You don't want to get a tapeworm do you?

Stella
Who else will eat it?
Let's finish it.
We're off now.

Ralph
And our plans don't include you.

Nick
Good luck!

He showers them with the scraps of the letter.

Stella
How did you do that?

Nick
Magic!
Will I ever see you again?

Ralph
We'll go into 'phone boxes in dark lanes.
Try directory enquiries. We'll track you.

Nick
It could take forever.

Ralph
One of these old days we'll find you.

Stella
Arrive at night!

Ralph
Steal your shoes!

Stella
Wake you up with a bucket of water!

Nick
Perhaps I should go ex-directory?
I don't need this night-nettling nonsense.
How will you call?
You could use the Roman coins!
I eavesdropped earlier.

Ralph
We'll call reverse charges.

Nick *blows his nose.*

Nick
I think I have a summer cold.
I'd like that, to convalesce.
Stay in bed, eat beans.
Let friends take me for walks.

Stella
It's time you went and changed.

Nick
Everything I want to do.
When shall I do it?
It's going to be a race.
All this to do.
It fills me up.

Stella
You have your moments.

Nick
If I had a camera I'd take a picture.

Stella
Now you have a memory instead.

Ralph
I'll return, when you don't expect it.

Nick
I might live in expectation.
How will you know?

Ralph
I came here tonight, didn't I?
Though I didn't know a thing.
Who you were,
or what was happening.

Nick
Where could I ever find you again?

Ralph
Where the eels scutter,
Where the mud is warm,
Where the cress is thick,
Where the newts squirm,
That's where you'll find me.

Nick
Goodbye my friend.

He goes.

Stella
Why did you lie to him?

Ralph
I couldn't say where we were going.

Stella
But he knew about the Roman coins.

Ralph
You have to leave people in hope.

Stella
He knew you were lying.

Ralph
As I said it I meant it.
He knew that.

Stella
You are an outrageous forgetter.

Ralph
It's better to forget what you don't wish to know.

Stella
Is that Julia?

Ralph
What will she do now?

Stella
She'll find something.
A thing all of her own.

Ralph
How can I leave her?

Stella
Forget it. You'll never see her again.

Ralph
She's upset. I'm upset too.

Stella
Don't lose heart.
Wasn't it you who said 'Play your cards quickly'?
This is our only chance.

Ralph
How can we go on?
How will it end?

Stella
We've got our lives.

Ralph
I have nothing.
So I may as well risk everything.

Stella
I knew you were going to say that.

Ralph
We each know what the other is thinking.

Stella
We want to watch these conversations
or we'll get married to each other in our heads.

Ralph
My sister, she's like me, she needs sex
and she's not been getting any I expect.
That's always at the root of these problems.

Stella
So what have you been up to all these months?

Ralph
Let's not talk about that.

Stella
How much of what you've told me tonight is true?
You can be cruel, I see it.

Ralph
At least I don't pretend to be nice.

Stella
That wouldn't be easy for you.

Ralph
I flatter myself less than her.

Stella
But you are.

Ralph *smells* **Stella**.

Ralph
Did you take the scent?

Stella
No. I picked up a bottle in the dark
and it spilt, all over the wedding dress
but that wasn't scent it was ink.

Ralph
Then it's the smell of you that I like.

Stella
You're like the sun itself.

Ralph
How? Smiling and even-tempered?

Stella
No. In a constant state of explosion.

Ralph
Then you're the moon.

Stella
What? Changeable you mean.

Ralph
No. Powerful and there's more
than you chose to reveal.

Stella
Shall we revolve around each other then?

Ralph
Let's do it!

Stella
I'll not tell you any more about me.
No one's going to know what's in my head.
It's where I am.

Ralph
Are you inside there now, looking out at me?

Stella
Yes: I like you, you amuse me and I'm curious.

Ralph
We were made for each other?

Stella
Do we deserve each other?

Ralph
Shall we have the wedding now then?

Stella
Yes; in the church, before dawn.

Ralph
Not marriage?

Stella
No, just a wedding and then off for ever:
into the new millenium!

Ralph
What kind of ceremony?

Stella
I'll pass the gentle man an apple!

Ralph
I'll bring the lady acorns in cluster!

Stella
We won't promise anything.

Ralph
Make the preparations silent,
for the pagan wedding.

Stella
You plant branches flaming in the lawn.

Ralph
You fill the church with mistletoe.

Stella
I'll wrap my bike in ivy.

Ralph
Then fold back the flower bed,
this is the end of two thousand years!

Stella
Complete.

He takes a firework from his bag, sets it in the turf.

Ralph
I'll need a match.

Stella
I've found a match.

She goes to light the firework.

Ralph
Hey Stella, we wrote a book tonight!

Stella
We need a book for the journey.

She lights it.

Stella
Kiss me now.

They kiss, take one look and go.

Nick *enters and watches the firework, then* **April** *enters too.*

[*Unless it hasn't gone off, then:*

Nick
An unexploded firework:
let me try my new lighter.

If it now lights:

Nick
I always get emotional when
I see these things go off.

April *enters.*

If it doesn't light, then:

April *enters.*

Nick
This firework, it's not gone off.

April
I always expect things to go up at any moment,
and they never do!]

Nick
The pagans, they took my watch,
my beautiful gold watch,
it was a wedding present,
or perhaps I lost it.

April
They broke my stick too,
or I could help you find it.

Nick
There's enough sticks here.
I could break down a sapling.

April
No. I hate to see a tree come down.

Nick
They should chop this lot.
It would clear the view.

April
Tonight: I feel anyone could have taken my hand, kissed me;

and we could have gone together in the darkness; like animals.
You and I perhaps?

Nick
No. I've had enough: it's a decision.

April
Why are you still here then?

Nick
Don't you know what's been going on?

April
No one knows what goes on.

Nick
What are you doing?

April
Washing my face in the dew,
on Midsummer's morn.

Nick
Watch where you do that.

April
Nothing's cleaner than the dew.

Nick
Not any more it isn't.

April
We have to live with everything that's growing around us.
You can't discard anything.

She picks up the scraps of the letter.

It all stays with us.

She hands them to him.

There's no unfinished business.
Don't you have children?

Nick
Not that anyone's told of; yet!

April
Only a man can know that.

Nick
No. Not know? Yes.

April
There was a woman,
looking for someone.
Do you know her?

Nick
Yes. Know? No.

April
Did anyone call your name tonight?

Nick
Not a soul.
Nothing turns out as I hoped.
Why?

April
The unexpected; it keeps happening.
Why not just accept it all?

Nick
Because I hate it.
Because the news is always BAD!

April
Perhaps it should be a triple principle?
The Untidy, the Unexpected and the Unexplained?

Nick
I see most people as either
unhappy, unmarried or unemployed.

April
If I still had that stick I'd hit you with it.
As it is I give you this.

She takes out a clover leaf.

I shall live gleefully now
because I have had my moment of vision:
a naked man in the forest

like a revelation he appeared to me,
stepped from the trees and spoke.

She gives him the leaf.

Goodbye Ralph.

Nick
Who's Ralph?

He laughs.

April
You didn't expect to find yourself here did you?

Nick
I chose it.

April
The light will come soon, I know it.

April *goes.* **Nick** *eats the leaf.*

Nick (*aside*)
A long night for a short one.

He picks up the dead firework.

I think Julia will be fine.
Tenacious, that's her nature.
It's the one thing that's endless.

He pours out the dust, then reads the name.

'A Mine of Serpents.'

A loud ambiguous sound: a firework or a gun fired.

What was that?
It's early to be shooting.
Or was it whoever did this?

The sound again.

Have the pagans gone?

He listens.

It should be the low ebb of the night,
but in spite of that

I can hear the gods walking
and the years turning.

Mrs Sparrow *flies in.*

Mrs Sparrow
What can be louder than time?

It thunders.

Nick
How are you?

Mrs Sparrow
Oh, I've been dead for years.

He drops the firework.

Nick
What?

Mrs Sparrow
I've come to warn you.
The next thousand years . . .

Nick
Yes?

Mrs Sparrow
The next thousand years,
it will happen.

A lightning flash.

Nick
Oh no!
But I only wanted a better day today.

Mrs Sparrow
You don't deserve an inch,
so I give you a mile.

Nick
But if we have no end,
do we have anything?

Mrs Sparrow
Your answer, it's the question.

Nick
Two thousand years done,

and I have lived as if there was no tomorrow.
Now there is one.

Mrs Sparrow
And there's another thing: about tomorrow.

Nick
What's going to happen tomorrow?

Mrs Sparrow
Tomorrow you'll wake up
and find you're alive.
Then you'll be sorry.

She goes. It rains.

Nick (*aside*)
After tonight,
I'll not come back here,
not walk these woods again.
These feelings,
I leave them here,
tonight.
Let the ghosts walk
I'll not see them.

Today: I'll get through it.

Time to be gone
but I'll not walk now
I'll run,
and I'll be waiting
for that call.

(*To the audience.*)
If the world's too big to love one person what can you do?

Birds sing.

He throws the scraps of the letter high into the air.

Once in a While the Odd Thing Happens

A Play from the Life of Benjamin Britten

Once in a While the Odd Thing Happens was premièred in the Cottesloe, National Theatre, London on 18 September 1990, with the following cast:

Benjamin Britten (b. 1913)	Michael Maloney
W H Auden (b. 1907)	Stephen Boxer
Beth Britten (b. 1909)	Hilary Dawson
Peter Pears (b. 1910)	Julian Wadham
Beata Mayer (b. 1912)	Deborah Findlay
One of the Chorus	Anthony Douse

Directed by Paul Godfrey
Designed by Stephen Brimson Lewis
Lighting by Paul Pyant

Scenes in England and America between the late 1930s and 1945.

Music
No music is required in the play.
Two pieces can be used set apart from the action:
The 'Romance' from *Variations on a Theme of Frank Bridge* Op.10 between Act One and Act Two, and the opening of *Four Sea Interludes* Op.33 to follow the final lines of the play.

Let me acknowledge the assistance of everyone who spoke to me on this subject especially Beth Britten (m. Welford), Basil Douglas, Joan Cross, Robert Medley, John Moody, Nell Moody (née Burra), Peter Pears, Myfanwy Piper, John Piper and Anne Wood.

Act One
England

1

W H Auden *and* Benjamin Britten

Auden
What I'd like to know is,
what goes on inside this head?

Britten
How do you mean?

Auden
Where does it come from, the music?

Britten
I was born on Cecilia's Day,
the patron saint of music.

Auden
But what is it; the nature of the gift?

Britten
Perhaps it was the rhythm of the sea,
heard distant as a babe in arms?

Auden
The North Sea, is it especially musical?

Britten
Do I disappoint you?
If I seem reticent, please don't think me dull.
It's simply that I run out of words.

Auden
Listen: you are the composer,
I am the poet, I am the one with the words.

Britten
I love your grasp of words

as if they were solid things
as if you could turn them round in your hands.

Auden
When I use a word it means what I choose it to mean,
but the eloquence of your music is another matter.

Britten
Why do people talk about music,
as if there was anything to be said?

Auden
Your music, it speaks directly to my heart.

Britten
And what does it say?

Auden
It begs questions.
All that emotion:
shifting and turning.
So much ambiguity.

Britten
You build me up.
I can barely follow this conversation.

Auden
You may act innocent
but the music gives you away.

Britten
Where is this leading?
If you understand, why do you need me to explain?

Auden
How do I know if the emotion I find when I listen
is what you mean when you compose?

Britten
What you hear is what I mean.

Auden
Doesn't it concern you,
that everyone may feel something different?

Britten
I'm sure they do.

Auden
What if no one receives your meaning?

Britten
Everyone has ears, don't they?

Auden
I envy you this absolute gift
but the ambiguity of it would drive me nuts!

2

Britten
I write music
every day,
nine till one
every day.
Inspiration
you can get it,
but what's more important
is to get it done.

English music
was nostalgic
that's the common view.
But I'm for something smarter
something sharper
something altogether new.

3

Beth *and* **Britten**

Beth
How's my favourite composer?

Britten
Help! Help!

Beth
I've got some news for you.

Britten
Help me.

Beth
What's this?
Is it thermometer time again?

Britten
I can't write music.

Beth
Then go for a walk
find inspiration.

Britten
No, I lost it completely.
My talent has gone.
I got up and found
I can't write music any more.

Beth
Nonsense.

Britten
It was a lifesaver
and now I don't have it.
What am I going to do?
I can't be a dentist like pop?
When I said I'd be a composer,
he said 'and what else?'
I should have listened.

Beth
You could teach,
most composers have pupils.

Britten
That's no good.
It's not good enough.

Beth
Are you discovering what it's like to be like
the rest of us, without talent?

Britten
My hands are shaking.

Beth
You could play the piano.

You're pretty good at that.

Britten
But I hate practising.

Beth
This can't be serious then.

Britten
I can't think of anything.
Perhaps I wrote too much, too quickly,
ran through all my ideas: threw them away?
I shouldn't've done all those films.
Why did I start so young?
Most composers don't begin at five.

Beth
God you bore me sometimes.
Perhaps you're being too ambitious,
trying too hard. Do a small piece.

Britten
I can't think how to do it,
how to start even. I can't remember what
it's like composing.
I've done some really good things.
How did I do them?
It seemed to pour out.

Beth
You've always said how difficult it is
putting notes together.

Britten
If there was a war now I might get killed
that would be best.
My early work would be thought promising.
I'd be a great loss to English music.

Beth
You can't talk like that.

Britten *is silent.*

Beth
What is it?

Britten
I've had a thought; out of my way,
let me go and try it at the piano now.

Turns back.

Hey, what was the news?

Beth
I'm going to have a baby.

Britten
Oh my darling sister!

Beth
It's seven weeks old; it has fingers and toes already.

Britten
You both came to the prom.
It must have been my piano concerto!

4

Britten
Nothing could be more insubstantial than this.

She says
'I'm having a baby.'
Meanwhile
I am clutching the walls like a bear
I am expending all my strength
to write some music
and it goes nowhere.
No one else does this exactly
so why shouldn't I have confidence entirely?
These are the choices I have made
and
my head is packed full of music
yet I find reluctance
when I should have purpose.
Meanwhile
she can
have a baby.

Nothing could be less substantial than this.

5

Britten *and* **Auden**

Britten
WHY?

Auden
Do what's asked then and
do what supports what you believe.

Britten
Serving causes?

Auden
There's less vanity in that,
and if people approve of your politics
they tend to like your art. Lots of people
do very well that way.

Britten
Little could be as wayward as you or I:
to make our living
by poetry and music.

Auden
It keeps us off the streets.

Britten
It seems no one wants us.

Auden
Why should they?
Most people are ignorant.
Most people have no taste.

Britten
I don't believe that.
It can't be true.

Auden
You're young.

Britten
Still, the BBC hardly play my music.

Auden
You know why that is.

Britten
The world is intent on destruction and
what use are we?

Auden
They need us.

Britten
How? Few people ever read poems
even yours.

Auden
Because no one will know
what the future will be.

Britten
Eh?

Auden
Because no one will know
what we need to know.

Britten
Yes.

Auden
How can we know how valuable
what we do will be?

Britten
No.

Auden
So they need you and me.

Britten
But I never know what I'm
going to do until I've done it.

Auden
This is why you are a special person.

Britten
Isn't it the same for everyone then?

Auden
You are the music

the pulse of our time is in you.

Britten
Why me?

6

Auden
The truth is
my tongue is
only loosely attached
and though I'd scarcely admit it
I do not hold
with most of what
I hear
from my own lips.

It is for this reason
among others
that I put the words
on paper:
to be
chosen expressions
of a capricious mind.

7

Beth *and* **Peter Pears**

Beth
Did you think it was all right?

Pears
I heard only good things
but then people tend not to say anything
if they don't approve. Don't you think?

Beth
I don't know.

Pears
What did you think? Did you like it?

Did you think it was good?

Beth
I'm not sure I know enough to say.

Pears
Go on. Tell me.
An intuitive response is always the best.

Beth
It felt confident and
I thought it seemed good,
of course it was over quickly;
I'd like to hear it again.
At the time you enjoy it and
then it's gone, difficult to remember
and grasp what it was after isn't it?
Did you enjoy it?

Pears
Oh yes. I thought it was incredibly exciting.
I don't know why but I expected it to be difficult
and it was so emotional.

Beth
It's a wonderful thing isn't it, music?
He's very clever, isn't he, my brother?

Pears
Goodness yes, I was beguiled.

Enter **Britten**.

Britten
They gave me flowers.

(To **Pears**.) Hello.

(To **Beth**.) Look, flowers. You have them.

Beth
Me? What a lot.
What should I do with these?

Britten
It's a lovely scent isn't it?

Beth
The flat will be like a florists.

Britten
Will you take them?

Beth
Do you want to talk to this gentleman for a moment?

(To **Pears**.) No doubt we'll meet again.

Exit **Beth**. *She waits at a distance*

Britten
They remind me of funerals.

Pears
Congratulations.

Britten
Thanks ever so much for coming.

Pears
Thanks for writing the music.

Britten
It takes a long time doesn't it?

Pears
What does?

Britten
To make a mark.

Pears
That was a very proper little note that you sent;
'When we meet next may I count you as a friend?'
You could have assumed that.

Britten
I don't presume it.

Pears
Why not, when it does another the credit of knowing
that you expect to like them?

Britten
Why expect to be liked? I despise that.

Pears
I only asked, because I was surprised.

I always counted you as a friend.

Britten
Perhaps I am not as certain as you think?

Pears
No one is. Best to act confident though.

Britten
Is that what you do?

Pears
What else can I do?
When I am told I have more expression than anything
I am told I am a singer with no voice!

Britten
Who said that? What rubbish people talk!
You write music too don't you?

Pears
No, I've not written any more music,
not since I heard yours.

Britten
Don't be too impressed.
I never expect it to work you know.

Pears
Then you can be affirmed if it fails
or pleasantly surprised when it succeeds.
Though in your case I imagine it's mostly the
latter, like tonight.

Beth *approaches.*

Britten
What a mess! And I've got to go now, my sister.

Pears
Tell me, why do you wince so?

Britten
Eh?

Pears
Do you find the world too bright?
Is this a rude question?

Britten
I don't sleep.
I lie there and think of music
and wait for the dawn.

Pears
I thought you were short-sighted;
only I saw you at the BBC, the other day,
gazing at us singers.

Britten
Then: I was listening to your voice.

Pears
Me? You could separate my voice
out of the whole choir.

Britten
Oh yes.
I've never heard anything like that before!

Beth *is there*.

Pears
So. You write music before dawn.

Britten
Not exactly. I have a routine.
I work in the morning and have a walk in the afternoon.
Sometimes, in London, I walk from Hampstead to the West
End, on grass most of the way.

Pears
Why not telephone me, next time you set out?
I could take a stroll across Regents Park
and no doubt we should meet halfway.

8

Britten
The city is full of young men.
I have been watching their eyes.
They have such coloured eyes.

Travelling underground

I see you
in a crowd
as I go by
but
the lines run parallel
and
I see you next
from a carriage window
in the other train.

We are hurtling into darkness
separately.
Why did you turn?
Why did you turn then?
Why did you turn to me?
I see your face in my reflection.

9

Pears *and* **Britten**

Pears
This wind!
I think I'm going to die.
It blows right through me.

Britten
Face this way.

Pears
Not likely.
Not in an east wind.

Britten
Come here.
Relax.
I'll turn you to face the wind
then open your eyes.

Pears
This is excruciating.

Britten
Can you taste the salt?

Pears
Can I turn back now?

Britten
Difficult to see those waves
and believe they're not angry isn't it?

Pears
If I get a cold you can answer to the BBC.

Britten
Which do you prefer,
the sunrise or the sunset?

Pears
I can't pretend I've ever been awake at sunrise.

Britten
What never?

Pears
No.

Britten
I can see you are a sleepy sort of person.

Pears
There's no denying you need sleep.

Britten
Even when I was a little boy
the light used to wake me in the early morning
coming up over the sea.

Pears
I'm not a great one for being awake at odd hours.
I prefer to watch the pink squares glimmering on
the wall in the later afternoon.

Britten
You never stay awake at night.

Pears
No, why?

Britten
Everyone goes into their rooms at night
and shuts the door. Is that it?

Pears
I doubt it.

Britten
It's not enough, at least if you
are awake in the night you know
there's life, that life continues.

Pears
If you're awake in the night
then you are hardly going to be full of life
the next day.

Britten
True, I have a cold bath in the morning
so that I know I am awake.

Pears
I can see you have it all worked out

Britten
No.
My father's idea of a holiday
was to get up at 4 a.m. each day and walk ten
miles. Is that eccentric?

Pears
There are people who sleep out under the
stars at night, who swim in the sea
at midwinter, for health.

Britten
Shall we do that?

Pears
When you are singing you have to
protect yourself. None of this would
be suitable.

Britten
Oh.

Pears
And there's the sea, it's not angry,
that's you being frightened,
though I should say it was beautiful
in a grim kind of way,
and I can taste the salt,

but whilst the bitterness of the wind
causes my face to glow
and I am grateful to you for bringing me here,
I think I should rather go back
and have some tea in the warm now.

10

Britten
Would you laugh
if I said
I'd rather be by the sea?

What can I tell you?

I am alone upon the beach,
the waves are at my feet
there is an onshore wind
and the rain tastes of salt.

I am watching the clouds
out across the sea
and the patterns of silver and grey
cast upon the deep water.

Nothing is familiar to me.
Was it yesterday I began?

My heart is beating out time.
There is no silence here.

11

Auden
I am the one
who walks into a building
and asks
when will this fall?
Who picks up a book
and thinks
how long will it last?
Who spots a child on the road

and listens for the cry.
Who sees the leaves on the trees
and waits for them to fall.
Who greets a clear sky
with an expectation of clouds.

12

Auden *and* **Britten**

Auden
How can it be so dark in the afternoon?

Britten *goes to draw the curtains.*

Don't draw the curtains.
Why not leave the curtains open?

Britten
I was going to put on the light.
It's just to stop them looking in.

Auden
'Them' Who are 'they'?
Are 'they' out there now 'looking'?
No one bothers to look in.
Leave the curtains.
Don't touch the light.
Let's sit in the dark
and look into the blue.

They sit.

Britten
Too much of this life is a mystery to me.
I only get a sense of things happening.

Auden
You give yourself away on a plate.

Britten
Me?

Auden
Speak.

Britten
This is how I am.

Auden
You should get analysed.

Britten
The world is too complicated already.

Auden
You'd discover things about yourself
you only dreamed.

Britten
Would it make life easier?

Auden
You don't want to know.

Britten
I'd rather be by the sea.

Auden
I've been thinking about you.
The desire to be at the edge of the water
this living on the edge of the sea
this trudging on the shore.

Britten
What about it?

Auden
I find it suspicious.

Britten
How?

Auden
Time you took the plunge.
The great ocean; of the Unconscious.
You are drawn to it.
It fascinates you, and you go paddling.

Britten
I go swimming.

Auden
You should go further.

Britten
I've been to Barcelona.

Auden
You've barely stepped out of the drawing room.
Go on a journey and see where it takes you.
Look at America.

Britten
I don't believe it exists.
I know it but I don't believe it.

Auden
Now there's a field for the imagination to go
roaming in.
Who've they had?
Whitman, Longfellow.
Well Whitman?
I can do that
I can do better than that
And on your side who is there at all?
Copland.

Britten
I've met him.
I like him.
I know him.

Auden
You can do Copland.
You can do better than Copland.
They need you. They need me.
We could really change things there.

Britten
Are you planning another visit across the Atlantic?

Auden
Not a visit.

Britten
No?

Auden
To be American.
Europe: the old country
the old world.

It's curling up like a dead leaf.

Britten
And you think America
is the answer?

Auden
Yes.

13

Britten *is writing music.* **Beth** *brings in a tea tray.*

Beth
I brought you the paper.

Britten
How I love Fridays
the *Spectator* and the *Radio Times*
as well as the newspaper.

Beth
Everyone's bored of reading
such bad news
except you.

Britten
Don't you want to know what's going
on? Who's been invaded, where
they are rioting in the streets?

Beth
I saw these people marching in the road
yesterday; everyone laughed.

Britten
Thanks for bringing me the paper.

Beth
Why do you think I brought you
the paper?

Britten *searches the paper.*

Britten
Oh God is there a review of the
radio piece?

Beth
No.

Britten
It's the announcement isn't it?
Thanks for making me a godfather.
I'll try to be a good one.

Beth
I always saw you as the family man.

Hands him a cup of tea.

Britten
I'll not rush in.
In fact I'm not sure if I shall get married
at all.

Beth
I know you better.
You like your home comforts too well and who
is going to do that for you if not a little wife?

Hands him a piece of cake.

Britten
They say the American girls are so pretty
perhaps I'll come back in a changed state?

Beth
It happens to everyone in the end
and you'll need someone to leave it all to
one day.

Britten
I'd love a little boy like your Sebastian,
but what if it was a girl?
And who should be the mother?!

Beth
There are enough wealthy music publishers
eager to wed their daughters.

Britten
But this year I am going to America.

Beth
Where did you get this idea from,

is it that poet? He's gone hasn't he?
A man like that is hardly a good example.

Britten
The King gave him a medal for poetry, remember.

Beth
I think he has lovely manners,
but some of these friends are so much older than you.
Is that how you expect to live?

Britten
There's a film.

Beth
A film, Hollywood?

Britten
Hollywood, yes. A film.

Beth
My.

Britten
It's the future.
What is there here? The old world.
And who've they had. Copland?

Beth
He had lovely manners too.

Britten
Europe: it's curling up like a dead leaf.
You only have to look at this.

Beth
I thought I would cut out the
Births Column.

Britten
That's a nice idea.

Beth
So you're going to do a film,
and visit Copland.

Britten
We thought we might stay with

him for a bit, yes.

Beth
We?

Britten
That's what we thought.

14

Pears
You and I
let us walk the moon's path
across the waters,
beneath your feet the waves
shall be a silver pavement
and lighthouses flickering all around
shall guide our way
over the sea
and under the winking stars.

Britten *and* **Pears** *leave.*

Beth *is left alone.*

15

Beth
In a placid house
at the sea's edge
there is still a child playing.
I sat silent
while
music rattled everywhere
and I watched the ships depart
for the deep ocean trawl.

Act Two
America

1

Britten
I am a young man in a nice tweed suit.
I am a fish out of water.
Either I was mad before
or I am mad now.
We're in America.
I saw a sign which said Suffolk,
Long Island.
There is no shingle here.
We are surrounded by lunatics!
We are living in a hut.
(It is in the grounds of a mental institution.)
I had a bit of music played
at a stadium,
five
thousand
people
came . . .
I apologised
when a piano wire broke:
They applauded my accent.

2

Pears *and* **Britten**

Pears
How curious it would be to be someone else.
I should like to know what that would be like.

Britten
That's an idle thought if ever there was one.

Pears
Can I try your shoes?

Pears
You can have these.

They swap shoes.

Pears
Hah, so this is what it's like!
Now we are each other.

Britten
How does it feel then to be Benjamin Britten?

Pears
Purposeful: I'd have to stand up straight in these.
Tell me about your new station Mr Pears?

Britten
Oh it's very comfortable, these are easy shoes.

Pears
What now?

Britten
Look at me.

Pears
Yes.

Britten
No. Focus your eyes on mine. Like this.

Pears
Hello.

Britten
Hello.
Don't laugh.

Pears
You smile only with the left hand side of your
face.

Britten
And the right hand side?

Pears
It doesn't smile at all.

Britten
Perhaps as I get older the smile
will spread across my face?

Pears
What now?

Britten
We just stay like this.

Enter **Beata Mayer**.

Beata
It's war.

Britten }
Pears } What?

Beata
They're having war. In Europe now.

Pears
Oh help!

Britten
We knew it would happen sooner or later.

Pears
I don't believe it.

Britten
I must write to my sister.

Beata
Thank goodness you two are here.

Pears
I can't go back now.

Britten
My sister must come here.

Pears
The boats are burnt,
good and proper.

Beata
The accidental refugees.

Britten
There's no choice now
but to remain and be American.
I intend to apply for citizenship.

Pears
Don't you think that's going a bit far?

Beata
You are welcome here, to stay
(Ignore what my father says).
I know you only came for the weekend
but I think of the hut as yours.

Britten
You and I; in that hut.

Beata
What have you done with your feet?

3

Auden *enters, déshabillé. He dresses.*

Auden
Speaking as an introvert
it's a joy
(to be anonymous is a rare delight)
but the crisis, I see it
as a long way off . . .

Of course everyone knows who I am
by now
and some of the company
is pretty attractive.

There's an open handed cruelty
to the heat:
in which
the old lose dignity
while
the young discover love.

I got the citizenship too.

So I'm not what I was any more
either.

Does this give you the picture?

4

Auden *and* **Britten**

Britten
Tell me your ideas for Broadway.

Auden
An Epic:
I thought we should do an epic.

Britten
An epic yes.
Musically, an epic would be terrific.

Auden
The subject is America.

Britten
But I don't know much about America yet.

Auden
You don't need to, you only have to write
the music.

Britten
That's lucky.

Auden
It's a very political subject.

Britten
That's good.

Auden
And the hero, the hero is the great American Hero
representative of the struggle of the people
and taller than the Empire State.

Britten
How do we do that?

Auden
He doesn't appear.

Britten
The hero doesn't appear?

Auden
I thought you could do that musically.

Britten
Musically that's a challenge.

Auden
And the heroine: she's a cow.

Britten
A cow?

Auden
Yes a blue cow
Babe the blue cow.

Britten
Your imagination it defeats me.

Auden
No, she doesn't appear either.

Britten
You want me to do that musically.
Tell me who does appear?
How does it begin?

Auden
It begins with trees. All these trees.
That will allow you to do choral writing.

Britten
For trees?

Auden
A forest: America – but not yet.
And there are these lumberjacks
and a telegram comes to summon them
to the task.

Britten
There could be a 'Western Union' boy
on a bicycle . . .

Auden
I like it.

Britten
And I can write the bell into the score.

Auden
I knew you'd catch on.

Britten
It's always an education to be with you.

Auden
Could you write 'Country' music?

Britten
You mean pastoral?

Auden
No.

Britten
Like in Westerns?

Auden
Yes.

Britten
I think I could try and
as an American composer I'll need to.

Auden
Remember, this is what we choose to make it.

Britten
These are such inspired ideas.
When are you going to write the libretto?

Auden
The book? I did it last week.

Britten
Genius!

Auden
The words await your music.

5

Pears
We went to stay at the house of the poet,
in Brooklyn.

You think you've stayed in strange places?
This one takes the biscuit.

At supper, between the stripper and the surrealist,
I didn't know where to turn . . .

There was a woman writing novels, a man in a tutu,
and everywhere the most dreadful Modern Art
leering at you . . .

It was a nightmare!

I was as polite as I could be until the day I found
a chimp in the bathroom. No one ever cleared up
either.
'Someone' replaced the telephone with a lobster.
and it wasn't only the stripper took her clothes off.

(A whole variety of unspeakable things went on.)

It
was
sordid
beyond
belief.

6

Pears and **Beata** *play catch with oranges.* **Britten** *sits on a rug. They eat the oranges.*

Britten
Don't you think it's important to experience
squalor at least once in your life?

Pears
No. Why? I did not come to seek the furthest
shores of Bohemia.

Britten
No one could be more fastidious than I
but all the same I love to be there when
he is spinning the words like plates.

Pears
Unwashed plates!

He has such strong imagination that when
he thinks of something he believes that's
how it actually is.

Britten
Isn't that what you call faith?

Pears
It makes him vulnerable to outrageous self-deception.

Britten
Every artist risks that, even you.

Pears
No, it's different for me because I am the instrument.
I have to keep in touch with that.

Britten
What about me then?

Pears
This is what the practise of music gives you.
I fear he is losing his sense of proportion.

Britten
It's too easy to make jibes at him
because he is so opinionated but he is just
about the most successful young poet in English
since Byron.

Pears
Exactly. Byron! Why do you idolise him so much?

Britten
What have you done?
Where are your ideas?

Pears
You know me I take things as they come.

Britten
An opportunist.

Pears
Even coming here, that was a kind of mistake.

Britten
I see.

Pears
I had engagements and planned to return.
You were the one following the poet's example.

Britten
I still maintain it was the best thing I ever did.

Beata
I could have died in Europe but I escaped.

Britten
So as events have shown it was a rather
inspired example wasn't it?

Beata
That poet, he's a bit of a pussycat isn't he?

Britten
His way of life may appear curious to some
but if you are a famous poet then it is
required of you to make bold choices.

Beata
My life is of no importance
and I'm quite happy. I relish the thought
of an ordinary life.

Britten
Oh I'm not an attention seeker.

Beata
Beth I'd love to meet her,
she sounds like a down to earth sort of person.

Pears
Did anything happen while we were away.

Beata
A squirrel fell down the chimney.

Pears
Do you mind us coming back to stay again?

Beata
My brother will be delighted.
It makes life more interesting for me.
My mother adores you and
father doesn't mind.

The hut would be empty otherwise.

Pears
We only came for the weekend the first time.

Beata
Think of it as a long weekend.

Pears
I have to take more lessons, do more work on
the voice and he needs a civilised environment
to compose.
He has to write a symphony to celebrate
two thousand years of Japanese Emperors.

Britten
Actually it's a requiem for my parents
and I like it here. It's clean and tidy here.

Pears
It's his first symphony.

Beata
You guys kill me.
All this self-laceration.
I'm so glad I don't have the need to do anything great.

Britten
It's not that.
It's just that he has the most interesting voice
of his generation.

Pears
You never said that before.
What do you mean by 'interesting'?

Britten
It interests me.

Auden *enters*

7

Beata
What will happen
to these three young men?

It's very important to them.
Such ambition
astonishes me.

I can tell you
I find the poems
obscure mostly
which is not to say
they aren't clever.
I look once
and
I look twice
and
the words swim.

I can tell you
I like to dance.
I adore shows.
Rhythms thrill me.
A strong tune
sustains me
working through the day.
Popular music
I love it.
This composer
doesn't rate it.
He switches the radio
off.

I can tell you
a natural voice
to sing,
that's a gift.
So why train it
if it makes you tense
all day?
Singing
it ought to be
a free thing
oughtn't it?

I do work hard
and treat people well
I try to be as generous

as I can
I think.
I am vulnerable.
I guard against complacency
I hope.

I find
the mere experience
of living
extraordinary.

It's obvious
each of these three
is a major talent.

It's obvious
each of these three
is unhappy.

Beata *and* **Pears** *exit.*

8

Britten *and* **Auden**

Britten
You have to admit, the show, (this collaboration)
it was a distinct non-success.

Auden
It doesn't matter.

Britten
Perhaps the hero should have appeared?
Perhaps we should have had the blue cow on stage?

Auden
No. It doesn't matter.

Britten
It there anything to be learned from this?

Auden
Yes. It doesn't matter.

Britten
What?

Auden
This is the great freedom you see
it means we can do as we wish.

Britten
You always have.

Auden
You can love people even if you disagree profoundly,
in fact I don't like people to agree with me any
more.

Britten
No. I mean, yes.

Auden
The colour of a man's eyes can be as important
as his opinions.

Britten
Is this the sum of your political thought?

Auden
Have pity. My best friend's gone off to join some
cranky religion and left me to a nineteen-year-old
college student.

Britten
But you still like it here?

Auden
Does anyone like to get what they want?

Britten
I've been thinking about London, the people in it . . .

Auden
London, it's just a city with everyone going round
to no purpose.
They hate you there – deserter!

Britten
. . . and my sister and my home. At each corner
of the marsh I left footprints. The winter will have
taken them away.

Auden
You're not talking about a place, you're talking about
your imagination.

Britten
You look at me, always with such expectation,
what can I give you that I haven't already?

Auden
What is it?

Britten
I used to collect things to tell you
so I wouldn't feel so inferior in your presence.

Auden
You were an innocent when you met me.

Britten
It was a long time ago.

Auden
I've taught you everything you know.

Britten
Poets, certainly, I've learnt a lot about
poets.

Auden
You mope and you don't say anything and then you
write this sensational music.

Britten
Why can't you let me be?
Why do you expect me to follow where you lead?

Auden
Didn't you choose to come here?

Britten
All this way to nothing.

Auden
You've had success here.

Britten
Nothing has changed.

Auden
You don't expect to change anything do you?

Britten
But you said . . .

Auden
Tell me what wisdom you think we have
to impart.

Britten
I'm writing music!

Auden
You can't pretend that altruism was
ever your prime motive.

Britten
What are we doing in this awful place?

Auden
I give you sincerity don't expect consistency as well.

Britten
There's nothing to look forward to here
except the winter.

Auden
Say something more for God's sake.

Britten
Can't, too full of thoughts.

Auden
I can see we shall need to continue this
conversation.

Britten *is silent.*

Auden
Don't walk away.
The worst thing you can do is walk away.

Auden *exits.*

9

Britten
I do not hear
what people say
but the sound of it.

I no longer see people

but I hear footsteps.

I do not look at the clock
but listen for dawn.

I would not need a map
to find my way
shorewards.

I know I am alive
I can hear breathing
and my heart
beating out time.

There is no silence here.

Britten *faints*.

10

Britten *and* **Pears**

Britten
Are you a St Bernard come to the rescue?

Pears
I've brought you a present.

Britten
Oh thank you.
I'm in need of something.
Hey, what's this?
An out of date copy of *The Listener*.
What use is this?
Is it a joke?

Pears
Read it.

Britten
I'm terribly ill and all you can do
is to bring me grubby old magazines!

Pears
Look at it.
It was found specially.
It has an article by E M Forster

about George Crabbe and 'Peter Grimes.'

Britten
Oh Crabbe – the Suffolk poet.
I know about him.
I've heard about him.
Give it here.
I'm very interested in this and
I'd like to see what Forster has to say too.

Pears
That seems to have perked you up.

Britten
I left as a prodigal
perhaps I shall die an exile?

Pears
Don't do that. Don't leave me here.

Britten
Everyone needs someone
to be like a brother to them.

Pears
Brother? Not like a brother.

Britten
No.

Pears
You have a brother in Wales, remember.

Britten
Do you think perhaps there's anything
we've not spoken of?

Pears
Yes. I think perhaps there might be.

Britten
I do too I think.

Pears
What am I to you?

Britten
You're my friend aren't you?

Pears
'Friend' that's a bit ambiguous these days,
sounds like a euphemism.

Britten
I see you as my partner.

Pears
Sounds like ballroom dancing or lawyers.

Britten
We're companions then.

Pears
Like 'companions in crime' or
something out of J B Priestley?

Britten
Accomplice, crony, sidekick!
I can't play this game.
The poet, he'd have a word.

Pears
Don't ask him!

Britten
Joke.

Pears
We both understand each other don't we?

Britten
Yes we do.

Pears
Then we can do better without any words.

Britten
That's good, now there's nothing we've not spoken of.

Pears
I'd do anything for you.

Britten
I'd do anything for you.

Pears
Be quiet then and read the magazine.

Britten
Yes sir.

11

Pears
Is he dying?
In my dream
I am walking with him
on a golf course,
in the distance
I see church towers.
How they sparkle!
The sky is luminous.
He is listening to the surge.
'The power of the sea is enormous'
he says,
'half the town has been taken away.'
Bells peal
and in my dream
I am holding him
as he is dying.

12

Beata *and* **Auden**

Beata
This is a surprise.

Auden
I've come to see him.

Beata
That's not possible just now.

Auden
We were in the middle of a conversation . . .

Beata
He's been near to death.

Auden
You're not serious.

Beata
Yes.

Auden
Why; is it to hit back?

Beata
For an incomplete conversation?

Auden
Psychosomatic I expect.

Beata
It wasn't psychosomatic it was serious,
I'm a trained nurse. I nursed him.

Auden
Still disappointed about the show perhaps.

Beata
What was this conversation?

Auden
If you'll listen I'll talk.
As you're here I'll talk anyway:
I can't remember what I said
but I was unhappy and therefore
I couldn't express that I was unhappy and
I think I was a little strident.
He looked unsettled.

Beata
Unsettled? His temperature went to a hundred
and seven.

Auden
Don't accuse me.

Beata
He was in delirium.
I sat with him.
He spoke for hours.

Auden
Did he mention me?

Beata
Not that I recall.

Auden
What did he talk of?

Beata *is silent.*

Auden
Does he remember?

Beata
No and I'll not tell anyone.

Auden
I knew he was concealing something.
I used to think it was a clear case of repression.
I expected him to break out in passion
and the composition to cease,
but that's not it, is it?

Beata
No. It's simply that he's so musical.

Auden
What does that mean, 'musical', it's not
like artistic or poetic is it? Or even tuneful
or melodious?

Beata
Any child knows what music is.

Auden
How can it mean anything if we can't explain
what it is? Here's this thing, the most abstract
art, yet with the strongest power to move our emotions.
How can he imagine it? How does he?

Beata
That accounts for all the walks.
He composes in his head then comes back
and writes it down.

Auden
But how?
I'd give anything to understand it.

Beata
It doesn't matter.

Auden
But I play the piano . . .

Beata
The understanding of music is like a taste for fish
or a preference for blue/green colours. Don't worry
about it.

Auden
I envy your sanity.
I admire you.
Such an entirely good person, if anyone deserves
to be happy it's you.

Beata
Shall I go make apple pie then?

Auden
I don't mean to be unkind.

Beata
Why do you need to admire me?
Why do you lot exclude me so utterly?
Emotion is democratic you know:
not connected to education or articulacy.
You don't hold the monopoly of intense
experience because you are a poet.

Auden
The truth is I've lost interest.
Life is rather disappointing isn't it?

Beata
Don't you have any faith?

Auden
I don't know. I think I have too great a
capacity for hope to be a poet.

Beata
That's not it.
Why are you so upset?
Did Ben mean a great deal to you?

Auden
Can I leave this for him?
It's the words of a hymn to St Cecilia.

Beata
You've cut your hand on the paper.

Auden
Yes.

Beata
I'll miss him.

Auden
He's not going to die is he?

Beata
No. He's better. He's with Peter somewhere.
Playing tennis I expect.

Auden
How are they?

Beata
Like two puppies: one yelping and the other
nodding his head constantly.

Auden
I begin to believe in the supremacy of music.

Beata
That's useless. A useless thing for a poet to
believe.

Auden
I put everyone's happiness above mine
anyone has more right to live than I.
Part of the day I work on giving the impression
of being in control.
Part of the day I think of how I can hold myself
together.
Part of the day I think of what I can do for anyone
else.
Part of the day I think if there's anything I can
achieve for myself.

Beata
What busy days you must have.

Auden
All I've done what use is it?

If anyone would take my life: I'd give it.

Beata
Poor man, you need to have some children.

Auden *laughs*.

13

Britten
The kiss
was unexpected
on both sides.
On the beach
I fix you
eye to eye
and
exchange a smile.
The kiss was unexpected
on both sides.

Britten *and* **Pears**.

They kiss.

Auden *sees it.*

14

Auden
From now,
from here
I am throwing away
all my hours.

From here
the years can fall away
for
I have
learnt too much
read too much
written too much
drunk too much
done too much

and
there's no doubt
I smoke too much!

The events of my life
I deny them.

This flat face
I take it
and tug it
tear it
twist it.

If
I have golden hopes of you
still
for the rest of my life
I shall be dying now.

15

Britten *and* **Pears**

Britten
What happened?

Pears
Has this not happened to you before?

Britten
I made the usual adolescent experiments.

Pears
Then I'll not ask you any more questions.

Britten
As I see you move now
I can feel the sensation
as if it was my own body moving.

Pears
Now I shall sit still then.

Britten
How can you be so alive
as if every bit of you was most you?

Pears
Perhaps it is by contrast
as I do not think I was alive until now.

Britten
I wish I could know what will happen.

Pears
You might not like it.
Let this be enough.

Britten
How is it possible to live today?

Pears
I shall sing.

Britten
Now that I no longer think I am going to die
it is quite difficult to know what to do
as I did not have to think then.

Pears
Why do anything today?

Britten
I always need something to do
else I get restless and
I would have wasted my time.
Shall we go for a walk together?
Perhaps I'll not be able to concentrate today
any way.

Pears
I had another astonishing dream.
So vivid and elaborate; and even more
extraordinary than that other I told you of.

Britten
You get all these dreams.
I've never had one in my life I could remember.

Pears
But you wake up with music?

Britten
While you were asleep . . .

Pears
You didn't sleep?

Britten
I had an idea.
I thought about opera.

Pears
Why now?

Britten
There's been none in English
not that I'd rate, not for two centuries.

Pears
How many hours have you been awake now?
And you're still recuperating.

Britten
I thought that's what I'd do.

Pears
What?

Britten
Do some.

Pears
Today?

Britten
When we get back
I'm going to do something else today.

Pears
You still need to rest, I need to sing.

Britten
I'll write you something.

Pears
For me? I'd die.

Britten
I'm sorry.

Pears
I'm pleased.

Britten
My face is sore from being kissed so much.

Pears
Mine too.

Britten
It must be miserable being a woman!

Pears
I can see we shall have to shave at night.

Britten
How are you now?

Pears
I'm well. I'm hungry.

Britten
My dear man.

Pears
My darling dear.
How are you now?

Britten
I'm well. I'm shocked.
I feel as if I had been in a car accident.

All the pieces of my body
seemed joined up in a way
that they are not usually.
And even fully dressed
I feel as if I had nothing on at all.

Pears
Are you really going to do what you said?

Britten
Yes, but time for breakfast now.

Pears
I'd like to wash first.
Do you think Beata will notice when we walk into
the kitchen?

Britten
Perhaps I should sleep?

Pears
What did you mean by 'when we get back'?

Britten
Oh Suffolk, you know.

Pears
Suffolk?

Britten
I mean the real one, not this pretend place.

Pears
That's what I thought you meant.

Britten
Suffolk on the other side of the ocean.

Pears
From now I live for you.

Britten
And I for you.

Pears
Don't move.

Britten
What is it?

Pears
There's a ladybird on your chin.

Act Three
England

1

Britten
I saw a light in your eye.
It was the single glint
in a dark cabin
that we shared.
The most intimate sparkle
in your watery eye.

Six months we waited
for a crossing:
it was early in the year
and the dread of icebergs,
took our minds
from the threat of submarines
and I composed
a Hymn to St Cecilia.

Between the engine
and the refrigerator
we slept.
Night and day
the engine turned.
We lay together;
face to face
eye to eye
silent in the depths of the boat.

2

Beth *and* **Britten** *and* **Pears**

Beth *waits, smoking.*

Beth
Ben!

Why didn't you tell me you were coming?

Britten
We didn't want you to worry.

Beth
You've changed.
Smarter I can see.

Britten
Where is my nephew to greet me?

Beth
Asleep. You look bad under the eyes,
that's where the illness shows,
and your smile is quite different
on both sides of the face now!

Britten
It's good to be here.

Beth
The film you went to do, it never happened did it?

Britten
Oh that, God knows.

Beth
How's the St Bernard?

Britten
You know Peter, he's a wonder dog,
and the barking is better still.

Beth
And no fights?

Britten
I've got him well trained.

Beth
Beata wrote, told me what happened.

Pears *enters.*

Beth
It was a long engagement?

Britten
Pardon?

Beth
Welcome Peter.

Pears
What I like about East Anglia
is the sky, it has such luminosity.

Britten
I should have known I could never
live anywhere else.

Beth
So why did you go?

Britten
Because I had to.

Beth
Had to?

Britten
I had to go to come back OK?

Beth
What does 'OK' mean?

Britten
All correct.

Pears
That's American for 'yes'.

Beth
And you wanted me to live there with you?

Britten
Not for long.

Pears
It was just to take care of us.

Beth
I can't take care of you two, I'm going to have
another baby.

Britten
Cor! Another one!

Pears
He's going to have a baby too.

Beth
What?

Britten
I am going to write the first grand opera in
English, set in Aldeburgh.

Beth
The first grand opera in English or
the first grand opera in English set in Aldeburgh?

Britten
Both.

Beth
When are you planning to deliver. I'm due in
January.

Britten
This'll take two years or more.

Beth
I've no doubt it'll outlive mine.

Pears
But perhaps yours will bring you more joy?

Britten
If we could do that perhaps we shouldn't feel
the need to do this?

Beth
I can't agree with you there.

Pears
Let us make music to smooth your way.

Beth
My mother had a craving for music
when she carried him you know. Strange isn't it?

Britten
I can remember being born: it was like the sound
of gas hissing.

Pears
Do you know what he used to say to me in America?

Britten
What yarn is this you're spinning?

Pears
'How I miss the fish and chip shop at Snape',
that's what he used to say to me.

Beth
It's an especially good one: local fish.

Britten
I could quite fancy a haddock and chips now . . .

Beth
I'll get them . . . (*She takes her purse.*)

Pears
No, let me, I'd like to. (*He puts it back.*)

Beth
There's no need . . . (*She takes it again.*)

Pears
Do you prefer plaice or haddock or cod? (*He blocks her way.*)

Beth
Small haddock and no chips then.
I'll give you some money.

Pears
Please, let this be my treat.

She offers money.

Beth
No. I'm welcoming you, remember.

He refuses the money.

Pears
Where's the shop?

Beth
Look I'll go after all.

She makes to go again. He blocks her way again.

Pears
No. No. Just tell me where it is.

Beth
But they know me in the shop!

Pears
Does Mozart like salt and vinegar?

Beth
Mozart – you call him Mozart!

Britten
Come on. Let's all go and buy fish and chips,
together, OK?

3

Beth
There are some things
I don't ask.
There are some things
between us now.

He takes the little boy
for walks
all around the marsh.
They bring me primroses.

I shall have three children.
I shall write no operas.
But I could write a book;
If I had the time.

It's a question of time.
It's a question of space.
It's a question of opportunity.
It's a question of knowing that you can.

Is this a new path for love?
I do not think so.

4

Pears *and* **Britten**

Pears *reads a letter.*

Pears
Prison. You realise this could mean prison.

Britten
I know we are unpopular but no one's
going to give us away are they?

Pears
No, not that, this.

Britten *takes the letter.*

Britten
The tribunal. I'll not be the first composer
to be imprisoned as a conscientious objector.

Pears
You are so stupid. Why did you say
you didn't believe in God and don't go to Church?

Britten
I don't; but I said I think Christ said
some good things that's what I think.

Pears
Not a very 'conscientious' objector are you?

Britten
I told them what I believed.

Pears
You are too honest!

Britten
I couldn't kill anyone not if you paid me.

Pears
That's not what it's about.

Britten
It's an issue of principle.

Pears
You do know how to make life difficult for yourself.

Britten
I refuse to accept this as a personal problem.
I prefer to see it rather as a social phenomenon.

Pears
Why should they listen to your honesty?
Time for compromise.

Britten
I'll not conform to some mean little bureaucrat.

Pears
So what's going to happen?

Britten
Vaughan-Williams is going to write a letter.

Pears
But you hate his music.

Britten
I often change my mind.
I'm sure I could find some that I liked.

Pears
And this is more honest?

Britten
I want to be left alone to write the opera
and I shall do some work for pacifist
causes but no compromise.

Pears
What about me? I compromised.

Britten
No one's going to snatch the paper from my hand now.
Little else matters but getting this done.

Pears
How much time we have wasted together.
All the time I used to have where has it gone?

Britten
I've never had time on my hands.

Pears
I don't think you ever really needed anyone.
I think you were quite happy before.

Britten
There's nothing I can say to you,
you know my thoughts.

Pears
I trust you.

Britten
And I trust you but I'm uncertain if I should trust
myself.
You know how good I am at saying the wrong thing.

Pears
Have less fear.

Britten
Hah! You see me . . .
I've never been more frightened than now,
but I'm happy too, with you.

Pears
I love the concerts that we do together.

Britten
No uncertainty there.

Pears
I've found my voice now.

Britten
There's little I could tell to represent my feelings.
I hear your voice singing in my mind.
It inspires me.
I construct music around that.
I put it at the centre of everything.

Pears
I give you my breath.

Britten
I suppose language does one thing and music does

something else altogether.

Pears
I would say music was your language.

Britten
You are the source of my joy.

Pears
There's so much of you I know hardly any of.

Britten
We've time, I'll tell you everything.

Pears
A certain degree of mystery
is essential to life, don't you think?

5

Britten *and* **Pears**

They change into evening dress.

Pears
How much time is there?

Britten
Just five minutes.

Pears
I have to lie down somewhere.

Britten
There's nowhere to lie down here.
What is it?

Pears
It's passion.

Britten
Goodness.

Pears
Passion overwhelms me and I hug myself
and have to keep shutting my eyes.

Britten
Is this the effect singing Michelangelo Sonnets
has upon you? Some say Michelangelo
wasn't you know and these love sonnets they
aren't either.

Pears
So no one can complain when I sing of my love
for you in public?

Britten
It's Italian, no one will understand.

Pears
My diction is good enough isn't it?

Britten
This is going to be a big occasion.
Do I look all right?

Pears
You look wonderful.
You always look wonderful.
You are wonderful.

Britten
Don't kiss me here, not in the Wigmore Hall.
I feel diabolical: sick again.
How's the voice?

Pears
I think I have a frog in my throat.

Britten
I still prefer you to any other singer
even with the frog.
Look at these hands, these are not pianist's hands.
I make mistakes.

Pears
The quality of your piano playing is rarer than
accuracy.

Britten
That's true!

Pears
You make it sound as if you had written it.

Britten
That bad, eh?

Pears
You turn everything round, no wonder
your hair comes out curly.

Britten
Would you like a drink?
Shall we have a drink?
Let's have a drink.

Pears
We'd better not drink now.
It would be good to have a drink after.

Britten
You're right. Thank you.
Thanks for stopping us drinking now.

Pears
When we get onto the platform, I'll follow you.

Britten
No. I'll follow you.

Pears
Oh dear.

Britten
Let's do what we always do.

Pears
See what happens.

Britten
Are you feeling better?

Pears
No. I want to touch you now.

Britten
Don't!

Pears
Are you nervous?

Britten
Me? No.

I threw up a couple of times. I'm not nervous now.

6

Pears
This is the moment when I am singing.
It's magical
As if I was
swimming in a pool
stretched out on the lawn
or
falling backwards into water;
but I have told you nothing.
It is
the best moment of my life.

Here are the songs of the long dead:
Dowland and Byrd and Purcell,
curious and beautiful names.

Your music now.
I feel you breathing
in here:
when I sing.
Your music now.
Here
I am.

7

Britten
All afternoon
I have been writing music,
the clouds moved fast
people walked by,
Peter practised three songs.
We slept
for a while,
drank tea
and I wrote pages and pages
of manuscript.
Then

I walked a mile
and came back:

An afternoon of early summer
has gone,
voices echo
in the house.
Voices echo in the air.

Enter **Auden**.

8

Auden *and* **Britten**.

Auden *is in US Army uniform.*

Auden
I don't know what I should say to you.

Britten
I'm sorry to be so incredibly late.
I was driving without headlights
it was embarrassing.

Auden
Embarrassing is a good word for it.

Britten
I wait for your words.

Auden
I don't know what you'd find useful to hear.

Britten
I still value your opinion above all.

Auden
If my other feelings are a mix
of inconstant proportions,
I carry hope and grief equally.

Britten
Speak.

Auden
Tenacity and despair fill me alternately,
but the vanity of my self-hatred
does not leave me speechless.

Britten
No?

Auden
There's little to you is there.
Your body is small
and those limbs tenuous.

Britten
How long are you in London?

Auden
I should be the ghost here
if I were not haunted by you.

Britten
Will you have much spare time?

Auden
Don't worry, I'm only here for one day.

Britten
I'd like you to see a performance.

Auden
I'm sorry about that.

Britten
You were always indifferent to attending the theatre
before.

Auden
I'd like to see your success.

Britten
It could be like last time.

Auden
This won't be like our last collaboration.

Britten
How do you know it will succeed?

Auden
To those of us who have known you,
we can see it is inevitable.

Britten
Thanks father. You don't know the struggle that's

going on.
Well, tell me then.
What did you think of what you heard?

Auden
In the end
I could not really say if I liked
or disliked it.
There it is.
Some of it I still think quite ugly
wilfully ugly.
Astonishingly beautiful I found it when
I knew you.

Britten
And now?

Auden
You've worked hard.

Britten
Yes?

Auden
It's there isn't it?
and it will be.

Britten
I'm going to write a lot more and better.

Auden
At least ambition doesn't colour my
dissipated life.

Britten
Pull yourself together.

Auden
Patronising snob.

Britten
I have to admit
I don't like you any more,
though I'll always have respect for your work
even those offensive little poems
you dedicated to me.

Auden
That was years ago.

Britten
It was bloody difficult.
How do you think I explained those to my mother?
Love poems? Your nerve in publishing them.
Why do you think I set them for women's voices?

Auden
Why do you think you are so important?

Britten
Why do you expect so much of me?
I'm just writing tunes.

Auden
I know the way you work.
I've seen it, and over six months
you get a lot of good ideas.
You work hard and put them together.
Your best ideas might constitute genius,
but you write out everything else as well.

Britten
I do what's asked of me.
A full time composer.
I'm here to be useful.

Auden
Rubbish. It's no excuse.
The sublime gift of music.
You treat it like a profession.

Britten
Don't you?

Auden
No. Poetry. A trade perhaps, but not a profession;
I know my place.

Britten
Can't you see I'm happy.
I've found my place now. This is where I belong.

Auden
It's where you belong all right.

Britten
That's important to me.

Auden
As if you could write music about a place.
As if an artist could ever have a country.
And music, music above all: that is just
itself and need refer to nothing.

Britten
You know
I never entirely understood your poetry,
I just wanted some nice words to set.

Auden
Has the ground opened between us for ever then?

Britten
I'm not frightened of anything now are you?

Auden
I can't answer that.

Britten
This is not a good way to finish is it?

Auden
Let's leave this conversation inconclusive shall we?

9

Auden
If my words are all I have to give you
let me say this
I could make a pretty garland

of nonsense

but I think you like plain words
so instead I choose adjectives,
just three,
for your music:

Mercurial

but eloquent

yet

uncomfortable.

10

Beth *and* **Britten**

Britten *is writing music.*

Beth
I've come to get you for supper and I won't take
no for an answer.
Have you done it yet?

Britten
One hour.

Beth
It's a long hour.

Britten
I'm stretching my time.

Beth
The roof's leaking again.

Britten
That's on account of the rain.

Beth
It's the age of the roof . . .

Britten
Peter's not back yet.

Beth
Why are you writing words?

Britten
This namby pamby writer I've got now is not much cop
so I'm doing a few bits myself just in order
to have it as I want.

Beth
I expect you miss the poet at a time like this.

Britten
Yes.

Beth
Did you ever see him before you left?

Britten
Oh yes. He was here too. I saw him briefly.
He was in fine form. America's been a big success
for him.

Beth
I suppose he must move in such elevated circles now
that we won't see him again, which is à pity
because I liked him very much.

Britten
It hadn't crossed my mind but I think you're probably
right.

Beth
Do you know it's Sebastian's birthday tomorrow?

Britten
Blimey I forgot; with Robert's pair I'm
five times an uncle . . .

Beth
Do you feel the responsibility?

Britten
I'd still like to have a child of my own.

Beth
If that's so you are choosing a strange way
to go about it.

Britten
Hmmm.

Beth
Soon, with peace in sight, I shall leave here.
Kit and I will make a home elsewhere.
Who will cook for you then?

Britten
I'll get a housekeeper.

Beth
I'll miss this place.

Britten
I'll sell it.

Beth
After I kept it for you all through the war . . .

Britten
We're going to live by the shore.
There's a house for sale on the front.

Beth
You'll be flooded out, drowned in your bed.
All it would take is a winter's storm.

Britten
Peter and I will sleep on the top floor as we do here.

Beth
If disaster strikes don't say your sister didn't
warn you.

Britten
Don't tell me how to run my life!

Beth
Sometimes I could shake you.

Britten
How do you imagine I felt when you married?

Beth
Perhaps as I do now?

Britten
Yes.

Beth
Kit, he's been away. I don't see him.
I might wonder which of us made the wiser choice.

Britten
What.

Beth
You needn't be quite so inscrutable.
As a schoolteacher I'm not ashamed to confess
there've been moments when I've felt stirred
by the presence of one of my pupils.

Life is full of ambivalent emotion.

Britten
I don't know what you're talking about.

Beth
I think you do.

Britten
What has it got to do with me?
I have been listening to the water dripping.
I have been watching insects fall from the roof.
I'm composing music here.
Thirty-five months to do this opera!
(I can hear your children shouting.)

Beth
I must get supper.

Britten
Yes.

Beth
Don't get me wrong.
I think such happiness is too rare to dismiss it.

Britten
I hear you.

Beth
If you knew what was going to happen,
what would you say?

Britten
I wouldn't believe it. No.
You must be joking.
All I have to prove is that it's possible
to live as an opera composer, because I need to
survive!

Beth
You'd better get on then.

Britten
What are you going to do?

Beth
Can't you see I've my hands full here,

with these three?

Britten
When they've grown, what then?

Beth
Me? I'm going to America,
to visit Beata; I like the sound of her
and I suspect we may have some things in common.

Britten
Goodbye Beth.

They kiss.

11

Beth
I never understood any of his music after that.
Much later,
in the spring
when I was seventy-nine years old
I met the writer of this
(which is how this play exists).

He brought me cigarettes.
I spoke.
We visited Shingle Street.
We came back to this house.

The leak in the roof is the same.
I did not go back again.
In less than six weeks
I died.

My brother.
My brother and Peter.
The poet.
My brother.
My brother?

Beni.

It's absurd to write an opera
in a war, isn't it?

12

One of the Chorus *and* **Britten**

Britten
NO!

Chorus
Mr Britten I thought you wouldn't mind
if I came and had a conversation, quietly.

Britten
I know what you want.

Chorus
This is nothing personal.
Please understand that many of us in the chorus
have liked your music in the past.

Britten
Thank you.

Chorus
I've come to say that at this moment of victory . . .

Britten
The end of the war.

Chorus
We feel a great opera would be better suited to
open the season with.

Britten
The decision has been made, you know that.

Chorus
I recognise the ambition of your work
but the music isn't easy is it?
We find it difficult to learn
and a punishment on the voices.
Even the orchestra are having problems.

Britten
I know. I know.

Chorus
There's simply not enough time,

and perhaps we shan't be able to give
our best in the circumstances. You see
it's essential to our self-respect
to know we can do that for you.

Britten
Can't you leave me alone?

Chorus
You have to admit that it's a big gamble
– that man hasn't ever directed before –
and if you look at it objectively there's never been
a successful English opera, not on this scale.

Britten
What do you want me to say?

Chorus
Don't you think it would be better to start with
something we know?
People want to hear lovely music now.
They crave the reassurance of the classic works.
It's a time of celebration and this opera of yours
it's a bit – well – it's a bit depressing isn't it?

Britten
Is there something I have to do?

Chorus
Perhaps if you had a word with Miss Cross.

Britten
She has resigned her position as director
of the company in order to undertake the role in
my opera.

Chorus
We can see how devoted she is to your music, but
we still respect her as head of the company,
if you relented she might see sense.

Britten
What the hell do you mean?

Chorus
You've had it all your own way.
We've seen everything.

Your precious opera with your 'friend' in the
starring role.

Britten
I don't have to listen to this.

Chorus
'Peter Grimes' is your first opera isn't it?

Britten
Well, yes.

Chorus
Then your arrogance is astonishing.
Why not think of the people who fought and won this war
who want a night at the opera now.
We have a duty to them.

Britten
I tell no one of this.
You never spoke – I did not listen.
This conversation it doesn't exist.
You do it.
You do it.
You do it.

Chorus
There's never any question of us not doing what's
asked.

Britten
You do it!

Chorus
Careful, you may regret this one day.
When we come to round up people like you.

Britten
I am not ashamed!

Exit **Chorus**.

(I am ashamed?

No.)

Here

I am.

Enter **Pears**.

Pears
You look dreadful.
You look feverish.

Britten
There was something.

Pears
What is it?

Britten
I can't remember.
It was a nightmare I think.

Pears
Can I leave you now?

Britten
Leave me never.

Pears
Are you awake?

Britten
I don't know.

Pears
Are you asleep?

Britten
I don't know.

Pears *hands him an envelope.*

Pears
There's a registered letter for you.

Britten
Thanks.

Britten *does not open it.*

Pears
You will see me before the show begins?

Britten
I'll be there.

Pears
Sleep now then.

Britten
Is this the world,
and am I in it?

Pears
Yes.

Britten
I'll be more awake later.

Britten *opens the letter and reads it twice.*

13

Britten
I sense a roaring
deep in the earth
and louder
than any sound.

It is on account of a letter.

I have been asked to go to Belsen
and play music:

Words do not encompass
my anticipation
of a death camp.

It is something more than this.

Neither dread nor dream nor fear
shall deflect
my purpose
to go.

I no longer
wonder
why I should
write music;
it's what's in me
to do
and nothing more.

I do this.

14

Britten *and* **Pears**

Britten
Are you ready?

Pears
No.

Britten
Have you been to the lavatory?

Pears *enters, in costume as 'Peter Grimes'.*

Pears
Yes.

Britten
At least you can do something.
I shall just lie at the back of the stalls and shake.

Pears
It's common knowledge that a bad dress-rehearsal
is a good sign.
Isn't it?

Britten
Let me tuck your sweater in.

Pears
But it's June.

Britten
This is how the fishermen have them in Aldeburgh.
Haven't you noticed? All year round.

Pears
They don't have to go under stage lighting.
Can you imagine what it's like?

Britten
I'm not you.

Pears
Why did you pick on me?

I can't do this.

Britten
Yes you can.
No one else in the world can do this,
as you can.
You have already.
Do what you did in rehearsal.
I wrote it for you, you know that.

Pears
Thanks.
Now I'm really on the spot.

Britten
Relax. I believe in you.

Pears
How are the company?

Britten
I don't think anyone has told them that hostilities
ceased a month ago.

Pears
I'm worried.

Britten
What is it?

Pears
I'm worried they'll lynch me in the lynching scene.

Britten
Remember it's only an opera.

Pears
You're no help.

Britten
I'm sorry.
How can you put yourself through this ordeal?

Pears
Because the truth is I am very strong.

Britten
Now there's fire in your eyes.

Pears
You knew it.

Britten
Peter: the rock.

Pears
What was the letter?

Britten
I'll tell you tomorrow.
Nothing to worry of tonight.

Pears
That's good.

Britten
This is only the beginning you know.

Pears
I know.

Britten
Did our director come backstage?

Pears
He came earlier. He said one thing and left.

Britten
What was that?

Pears
He said:
Whatever happens next we were right to have done this.

15

Britten
Even before I wake
there's music
I am lying suspended in it
until
a sleepy moment
when
I find
the subsidence of sound

and
awake
into silence
before I am invaded
by a memory of music
I have not written
yet.

Afterword

Beth Britten's contribution to *Once in a While* . . . . .

When I set out to write this play I was inspired by the idea of exploring the dramatic force in Benjamin Britten's music. Originally I intended to write some kind of response to this but it was only after meeting several of Britten's contemporaries, and in particular his sister Beth, that I stumbled across the real drama.

I met Beth in the last six months of her life. She knew she was dying although I did not, and she insisted that I spend a month of the early spring of 1989 with her staying near her home in Aldeburgh and going over to talk with her each day.

Of the four Britten children Beth and Ben were the youngest and they developed a powerful and intimate relationship in childhood. Beth was not sentimental about Britten and was if anything critical of what she saw as 'precious adulation' by those who had never met her brother but who referred to him by his first name, even after his death. He was to her firstly a brother secondly the great composer.

'The first thing you must understand about my brother,' she told me, 'was that he was essentially a family man.' Now Britten was not what was commonly understood as a family man, even though it is true he always needed the protection of a group of people around him.

With this, as with much else, it was necessary to reinterpret what she told me. She had a profoundly subjective view of her brother and there were certain areas, notably his relationship with Peter Pears, that we did not discuss. Yet this taboo told me a great deal.

Britten had been a sickly child, the doctors had recommended a hospital school, but his parents had rejected the idea preferring to bring him up as a normal child. This was far from possible because he began to write musical notes, mastering these before the written word. Music was such a dominant force that no one was allowed to play the piano in the house after he had gone to bed or he would wake and cry.

Beth and her brother both chose to idealise their childhood yet Britten's work betrays a preoccupation with innocence corrupted or threatened. I believe that the dark side in his personality reflects the events of his childhood.

Though already frail, Beth had immense reserves of energy and insisted we visit the places she had known with her brother and Auden. We visited the Old Mill at Snape several times. We walked from room to room as she described how it had been when she had lived there with Britten and Peter Pears until 1945 when her husband was demobilised and they made a home elsewhere.

While Beth had been fond of W.H. Auden 'He had such lovely manners' Pears was 'that man'. The profound relationship in Beth's life had been that with her brother, and while she accepted Pears' existence and the relationship with Britten, there was a tension between the two.

When Hilary Dawson, the actor who took the role of Beth, visited Sally Lange Beth's daughter she learnt that during her whole childhood Sally had never once seen Britten and Pears touch, nor had it ever crossed her mind that there had been any relationship between them. They all existed together in the long damp corridors of the converted Old Mill in apparent peace.

Only once did Beth let me behind the veil and then it was by her silence. We stood in a studio where Britten had composed *Peter Grimes* and there was just one room left to visit, the upper room where he slept. I suggested we went upstairs. 'No,' she insisted, 'I never went up there!'

Yet she spoke eloquently of those times when Auden came to stay and was packed off to sleep in the dampest part of the house. She recalled noisy family meals with Britten bent double straining to listen to the radio above the shouting of Beth's children.

After 1945 until the last year of Britten's life there was a rift. Whilst he was absorbed into the world of music Beth was occupied with her family. 'I never understood any of his music after that.'

Beth died six weeks after I last saw her. Many months passed before I learnt this. It was only when the play was nearly complete and I wrote to ask if she might wish to read it that I discovered she was gone.

The Blue Ball

'. . . the fortune of us that are the Moones men doeth ebbe and flow like the Sea, beeing governed as the Sea is, by the Moone.'

Henry IV, 1

'I didn't go into space just to return and open supermarkets.'

Helen Sharman

Characters

Alex, *the best pilot (20s)*
Dan, *a pilot (20s)*
Stone, *the top scientist (50s)*
Carl, *a pilot (20s)*
Sylvie, *an astronaut (30s)*
Paul, *the playwright (30s)*
Anna, *Alex's wife (20s)*
Roger, *an astronomer (30s)*
Judy, *a doctor (30s)*
Bob, *an astronaut (40s)*
Nell, *Bob's wife (40s)*
Oliver, *an astronaut (60s)*
Gina, *an actor (40s)*
Several pilots

The research scenes take place in America in the present day while the other parts of the play refer to a time thirty years before. I wish the audience to understand that the scenes with Alex take place within a space programme that's neither American nor Russian but something created by the playwright: a synthesis of the two.

The Blue Ball received its première at the Cottesloe Theatre, Royal National Theatre, London, on 23 March 1995 with the following cast:

Alex	Dexter Fletcher
Dan	Mason Phillips
Stone	Nigel Terry
Carl	Nicolas Tennant
Sylvie	Annabelle Apsion
Paul	Peter Darling
Anna	Pooky Quesnel
Roger	George Anton
Judy	Sonia Ritter
Bob	William Armstrong
Nell	Gabrielle Lloyd
Oliver	Trevor Peacock
Gina	Annabelle Apsion

Directed by Paul Godfrey
Designed by Stewart Laing
Music by David Sawer
Lighting by Mimi Jordan Sherin

1

Several pilots including **Alex**, **Dan** *and* **Carl**.

Several pilots
Now we are going to find out the truth.
Which of us is it to be?
The man knows.
I know.
We all know, everyone knows.
Each of us thinks it's him.

Alex
I don't know, I have no idea.

Dan
It could be any one of us.

Stone *enters*.

Stone
Here's the decision. (*Picks* **Alex**.) It's you.
(*Picks* **Dan**.) And you will be the standby.
(*To* **Alex**.) What's your reaction?

Alex
I'm pleased . . . I'm grateful.

Stone
You must never be grateful
because we're not being generous here.

Alex
It's all I hoped.
Everyone looks to the sky.

Stone
You've no fear?

Alex
I know there's the possibility of that emotion
but I've learnt to overcome it
(unleashing a blind panic can risk the success of a flight
and endanger the lives of others).

Stone
Aren't you frightened of death?

Alex
When I became an airman I found I could accept death.
It surprised me.

Stone
You have children don't you?

Alex
Yes, to be here when I'm gone.

Stone
You don't value your existence very highly?

Alex
Whether I live or die you offer the chance of something else.

Stone
So you are prepared to stake your life?

Alex
I am happy to do this.
You need the best pilot.
I understand that.

Stone
All I need at this moment
is for you to believe this.

Alex
I believe it.

Stone (*to the others*)
When he succeeds you will all be next.
Everything will be possible
once we have done this.
For the next thirty-six hours
you two will prepare,
both of you will go out onto the launch site
and only then
will one step forward.
Now you all have one last duty together
before we part here
and that is to record this moment.

They line up for a photograph.

Dan (*aside*)
Even if it was a sentence of death
he seemed happy and unware.
For thirty-six hours
as his shadow
I began to believe
I was him.
I saw no difference between us.
We both had the same training.
I couldn't figure it out.
Why was it him and not me?
I was angry with envy.
When it came to the moment
I nearly stepped forward
that's how close I came to it.
I was surprised to find myself walking away.
Later when they fired the rocket
there was an inferno of flames
and I was sick with relief.
On the radio he was laughing.
I was glad to be safe.
Thank God they didn't pick me.

Carl (*to* **Alex**)
We wish you well.
We count this no dishonour
because we are all your friends here.
We were proud to know you.

Alex
Thank you.
I'll take your names with me.
You must all sign a piece of paper
and I'll put it in my pocket.
Now, let's begin. I know what to do.

Exit **Stone**, **Alex** *and* **Dan**.

Carl
Who wants to make a bet?
No?
I don't believe it can work either.
Now we are going to find out the truth.

2

Sylvie *and* **Paul**.

Sylvie
I admit it, I am ordinary.

Paul
You're the first astronaut I've met.

Sylvie
There's nothing special about me.

Paul
What is it like in space?

Sylvie
Being in space, I'd say it was
more incredible than you could imagine . . .

Paul
So what surprised you?

Sylvie
Everything.
Nothing could prepare you for that.

Paul
Can you be more specific?

Sylvie
Yes, the *whole* experience was a surprise.

Paul
In this play what must I show?

Sylvie
You've got to tell them about the wonder of it,
how overwhelming that is.

Paul
Do you talk about it much,
have you given many interviews?

Sylvie
Are you kidding?
We're trained to talk in soundbites here.

Paul
I am not a journalist
you can tell me whatever you want.
Why not talk about your emotions?
You said it was overwhelming.

Sylvie
Yes, but there's no room for emotion in space.

Paul
Isn't wonder an emotion?

Sylvie
Emotions are irrelevant to an astronaut.
If you were to think about it you could feel helpless.

Paul
You learn to deny emotion?

Sylvie
It has its place, afterwards.
You should see our touchdown parties.

Paul
I'm glad I met you first.

Sylvie
Why?

Paul
Because you're a woman.

Sylvie
So?

Paul
Do women have a different view of space?

Sylvie
Gender and race aren't issues here.
I don't see myself as a woman.
Being an astronaut is more significant
than any racial or gender difference.

Paul
It's simply that I know most astronauts are white and male.

Sylvie
NASA tries to be an equal opportunities employer.

Paul
Except when it comes to moon landings?

Sylvie
Look, if you know what it is you want to learn,
then ask me and I'll tell you.

Paul
I don't have an answer to that.
Whatever I find I can use
but writing a play is primarily an act of the imagination.

Sylvie
Is that so?
I'm not ashamed to admit that I have no imagination at all.

Paul
I don't believe you.

Sylvie
We work to fulfil the expectations placed upon us.
Imagination is not one of them.
We're trained to analyse a situation then act,
to think and then speak,
but I admit this is a new situation for me
talking to a playwright.

Paul
How can I grasp this experience you've had?
It's a wonder to me.
Talking about it here now, it seems unreal.

Sylvie
Why should anything be more wondrous
than anything else?
Why should it be more wondrous for me to go up in orbit
than to be here having a conversation with you?

Paul
Here we are in a room,
there you were out in space.

Sylvie
Here we are.
There's a sense in which we are in space now.

Paul
Travelling through space now.

Sylvie
Exactly, it's a wonder we can stand up at all isn't it?

Paul
That's true, but it's commonplace;
your experience is new entirely.
That's what I want to know about.

Sylvie
Look, I'm doing my best
I'm telling you about me,
what I'm like;
and what it's like in space.
Aren't you getting a picture now?

Paul
Let me try a different question.
Do you like it in space?

Sylvie
Me, I would go even if I could never come back.

Paul
I've never met anyone like you.
Are you famous?
Do people recognise you in the street?

Sylvie
Now and again people recognise me here,
there are so many astronauts around
but elsewhere no one would pick me from a crowd,
there's nothing extraordinary about me.

Paul
Isn't there?

Sylvie
WHAT?

3

Anna
We rise in the dark
and he leaves me in the dawn.
Each morning I am full of hope
even if the routine is mundane.

I didn't have many choices,
I knew marriage was inevitable,
I left home and went to a typing school.
That was my bid for freedom.

We met the pilots at the base.
They knew we were easy
but I wasn't that interested
so I became a prize
then I was able to choose between them.

I got the best pilot,
and everyone hated me for it.

Alex *enters*.

Alex
It's me they've picked.

Anna
I knew it.
I needed this.

Alex
We worked hard.

Anna
I dreamed of flight.

Alex
Now we've got something,
it's been worth it.

Anna
We made every sacrifice.
I never had anything.

Alex
Are you pleased?

Anna
Everyone will treat us differently now.

Alex
Need they?

Anna
They had better.

Alex
I met the top scientist.
I knew I could trust him instantly.

Anna
I'm so happy.

Alex
We can't tell anyone.

Anna
I don't mind not telling anyone
because we'll be rich.

Alex
Don't be petty.
I'll get no more money.

Anna
Not yet.
But the day will come.

Alex
Will it?

Anna
What shall I tell the children?

Alex
Tell them their father is an extraordinary man.

Anna
I knew you were unique.

Alex
I'm unique now.

Anna
When is it?

Alex
Tomorrow, after midnight,
less than thirty-six hours.

Anna
What shall I do?
How can I be ready?

Alex
Now I've told you,
now I have to go.

Anna
What if you don't come back?

Alex
I don't know.

Anna
What's going to happen?

Alex
I don't know.

Anna
I'm never going to see you again.

Alex
No.

Anna
Kiss me.

Alex
Don't squeeze the life out of me!

Anna
You've plenty of life in you.

Alex
Goodbye.

Anna
What's to become of me?
Don't go.

Alex
Don't be frightened.

Anna
I'm not frightened, I'm greedy for you.

Alex
I'm not frightened either.

Anna
You're mad then.

Alex
I'm lost?

Anna
Not yet.
Go.
Go and come back.

Alex
I'll go and come back just the same as I am now.

Exits.

Anna
If they kill him could I manage to start again?

4

Paul, **Roger** *and* **Judy**.

Paul
Here are the phone numbers of all the Apollo astronauts:
who shall I call first?
Shall I call Neil?

Roger
Neil? Don't bother.

Paul
Shouldn't I talk to Neil?

Roger
No, I should forget him.
Cross him off the list.

Judy
Why do you want to meet astronauts,
they're merely human like everyone else aren't they?

Roger
Neil Armstrong gave a lecture at the astronomy faculty.
He spoke for two hours about the moon
and never mentioned that he'd been there.

Paul
I had the chance to travel, a small grant,
and I thought who in the world would I most like to meet.

Judy
Now you've met one; what was he like?

Paul
She, she was extraordinary.
She said she had no imagination.

Roger
Did you ask what it was like in space?

Paul
She said it was more incredible than you could imagine.

Roger
Wow.

Judy
It can't be difficult for something to be more incredible than
you can imagine when you have no imagination.

Paul *dials.*

Paul
This is Alan Bean, the astronaut who's taken to painting,
perhaps he'll understand what I'm about?

Judy
Why should an astronaut be more interesting than anyone
else?

Paul
I want to know about the experience of being in space.

Roger
You need to learn some astronomy.

Paul
OK, explain what it is you do exactly.

Roger
I work in the search for the missing matter.
You know that most of the mass of the Universe is missing?

Paul
He's not there. No?

Roger
We can see what there is where there's light
so . . .

Call answers.

Paul
(Hello. This is Paul Godfrey.
Did you get my letter?)

Roger
. . . I look where there's darkness
where there doesn't seem to be anything.

Paul
(I'm here researching a play
and I'd like to come and talk to you.)

Judy
There are plenty of actual wonders he should take in.

Paul
What's an actual wonder?

Judy
The Grand Canyon
or the Niagara Falls
or even the Great Plains.

Roger
That 97 per cent of the Universe is missing.

Paul
(Can I come and talk to you while you're painting?)

Roger
We know it exists but no one can find it.

Judy
You go there and you still can't believe it.

Paul
(I am interested in how astronauts behave before and after
they've been in space.)

Judy
Something like that you can't hold it all in your head.

Paul
(I want to see how your paintings communicate what it's like
in space.)

Roger
I believe that what we can't see must be somewhere we can't
see it.

Paul
(No, there's no budget to pay you a fee.)

Roger
So I am hoping I might just find something.

Judy
You mean 'nothing'?

Paul
(I've nothing like that kind of money.)

Judy
It wouldn't be *anything* would it?

Paul
(Let me buy you lunch.)

Judy
Not if you look where there's nothing.

Paul
(Don't you take a break?
Why not have lunch?)

Roger
But if I found it it would be something.

Paul
(But if you can eat while you're painting,
why can't you talk while you're painting?)

Judy
If you can find something where there's nothing
then that would be an actual wonder.

Paul
He cut me off.

Roger
Are you disappointed?

Paul
Well no, I talked to a man who walked on the moon.

Judy
Did he say anything good?

Paul
You heard the conversation.
It was either buy a painting or pay a fee.

Judy
I work with a woman who's married to an astronaut,
I'm sure you can meet him
while you are staying with us.

Roger
I'd be interested to meet an astronaut too.

Paul
Could I talk to both of them?

Roger
Let's all do dinner.

Judy
OK, I'll call her.

5

Anna *and* **Stone**.

Anna
Is he here now?

Stone
Yes. In a moment he'll come

and you can have a few minutes alone.
Now we need to talk first.
It's this: if he has any after-effects you must tell me.

Anna
Will he be changed?
Is something wrong?

Stone
No. I believe he will be unchanged
but I don't want him to hold anything to himself.

Anna
He's honest.
He's an honest man.

Stone
If there are any ill-effects, I must know.
You must tell me;
but we don't want him to feel uncomfortable
so I don't want him to know this.

Anna
I understand.

Stone
It's in his interest.
It's in all our interests.

Anna
All that matters to me
is that he's still alive.

Stone
He's alive. Are we agreed?

Anna
Yes.

Alex *enters with blood on his face.*

Alex
I am the luckiest man alive.

Stone
My children . . .

Stone *exits.*

Anna
Is this your hand?

Alex
Yes, I hope so.

Anna
Is this your body?

Alex
Yes, I think so.

Anna
It's you, I'm sure.

Alex
An orbit of the entire earth
in a hundred minutes of my life.

Anna
What was it like?

He looks at her.

And you're safe?
You're shaking.

Alex
I'm here.
I can just stand
but I can feel the gravity pulling me down.

Anna
God.
Did you see God?

Alex
No, but I looked.

Anna
If you didn't see Him then where is He?

Alex
It was a small window, I had a camera, but no telescope.

Anna
Did you see the stars?

Alex
Yes. And the moon too.
The sun rose twice.

Anna
I thought you would die.

Alex
It all worked well enough.

Anna
Our children are asleep.
Everything is as it was.

Alex
Everything happens once doesn't it?
Only once for the first time:
this is that moment.

Anna
It's not in everyone's destiny to get a glimpse of heaven.

Alex
I saw the world turning.

Anna
Does it revolve like a school globe?

Alex
Yes.

Anna
Who could believe that?

Alex
I believe my eyes.

Anna
Tell me about the stars.

Alex
They don't sparkle.

Anna
How is that?

Alex
It's the sky that diffuses the light.

Anna
It's not real then?

Alex
Does it matter?

Anna
I need to believe my eyes too.
Tell me is the earth green?

Alex
It's blue.

Anna
Like the sky?

Alex
Like the sea.

Anna
How? Water has no colour.

Alex
The sky itself is transparent from above,
I saw the blue sky reflected into the blue sea.
From space even the sun is a bluish colour,
not yellow at all.

Anna
In an hour the sun will rise.

Alex
No.

Anna
The sun always rises.

Alex
The sun never rises.

Anna
What then?

Alex
The earth is revolving.

Anna
You said the sun *rose* twice.

Alex
I did, didn't I?
That shows how quickly you can forget.

Dan *enters*.

Alex
I'm telling her what I saw.
All these things competing with each other.
How can I separate the thoughts from the sensations
and the sensations from the sights
and the sights from the thoughts?
How will there ever be the words
to disentangle them all?

Anna
My heart is beating like a drum.
I tell you, I shall look at the sky differently now.

Alex (*to* Dan)
Here's the paper, here are your names
that I took with me.

Dan
The same piece of paper.
We won't divide it, we'll keep it whole.

Alex
Nothing in my life can ever match this.

Stone *enters*.

Anna (*to* Stone)
He looks no worse than he did sometimes
after what he suffered in training.

Stone
I rely on you to create a normal existence for him.

Alex
I'll be myself again soon.

Stone
I'd like you to have more children
prove to the world you are still a man.

Alex
Back for the rest of my life.

Dan
And now it begins.

6

Judy, **Bob**, **Nell**, **Paul**, **Roger** *in a restaurant.*

Judy (*aside*)
Perhaps I am the only person in this town
who doesn't want to go into space?
It holds no interest for me.

Perhaps you wonder how I get on with him
when his universe is at the end of a telescope
and mine is here and now?

Perhaps you noticed
I am not a tolerant person?
It isn't in my nature.
Tolerance is not admitting you disagree;
I disagree, that's my nature.

Tolerance is a meagre virtue,
I prefer generosity
because that's bigger.

All of which means
simply by arranging dinner
for this playwright to meet an astronaut
I am able to feel good about my intolerance.

Bob (*to* **Paul**)
You must understand that though I am an astronaut
I still am an essentially ordinary man;
it's simply that I have been lucky enough to do some
exceptional things.

Nell
We never met a dramatist before.
Tell us what you write about.

Paul
My last play was about music.

Roger
Before he begins his questions there was something
I wanted to ask Bob about the Challenger.

Nell
Music is a good subject.

Bob
That was a grim business.
They were all my friends.
We trained together for years.

Nell
It could have been him,
it was luck, he wasn't selected for that crew.

Bob
I love music, I like to listen to Handel
when I am in orbit.

Nell
I expect you can see now
how we could be anybody.
I could be the wife of a pilot, or a cop, or a diver.

Judy
That's what I said (forgive me Bob),
why are astronauts interesting?

Roger
The shuttle wasn't destroyed was it?
I heard they dredged most of it up.

Paul
I am interested, that's enough for me.

Nell
The one about music, I'd like to see that.

Bob
The booster rocket exploded
but the shuttle was completely intact
when they took it out of the ocean.

Roger
And the people inside . . . ?

Bob
They were there.

Judy
Beats me to see why this is interesting,
when there are an endless number of people and stories
you could choose from?

Paul
I am interested in science and technology
and to me the space programme represents
the peak of technological aspiration.

Bob
He's right.

Nell
I love the theatre.

Roger
What happened to them?

Bob
They were liquefied.
The vibration and high pressure
reduced them to human jelly in their flight suits.

Roger
What a death,
and it could have been you.

Bob
That's what I thought.

Nell
I never heard this before.

Roger
Only bags of bones?

Bob
No bones left.

Judy
Do you need to know this?
We've just had dinner!

Bob
Could you put that in a play?

Paul
Anything's possible in theatre.

Nell
They wouldn't have known anything would they?
It must have been instant, wasn't it?

Bob
Not necessarily, as the temperature and pressure built up
they may have lost consciousness
but they could have taken as long as eight minutes to die.
We'll never know exactly.

Judy
Isn't there a safety procedure?

Bob
We rehearse bailing out
but we could never do it at that speed.

Roger
A one-way ticket.
When you've got a mission coming up
doesn't it frighten you?

Nell
He has one in twenty-six days.

Bob
You learn all you can
so you know the risks
and then you accept that.

Nell (*to* **Paul**)
Are you going to go to the theatre while you're here?

Paul
What should I see?

Roger
The film of *The Right Stuff* is being shown.
You should see that.

Bob
No one understands how dangerous the space shuttle is.
There are millions of things that can go wrong:

we rely on every instrument to work at its peak capacity
yet each flight reveals hundreds of new flaws!

Roger
So it could go bang at any moment of the flight?

Bob
On our last flight the outer windscreen was damaged,
hit by a flake of paint less than a millimetre in size.
The atmosphere is getting more cluttered
and the risk is growing all the time.
Pieces of space junk collide and divide in orbit
creating more and more bits of debris.

Roger
So at that speed a large piece could destroy the shuttle?

Bob
Yes.

Nell
Perhaps your play about astronauts will be done here in
Houston?

Bob
You should visit the Opera House.
We went to the première of Michael Tippett's *New Year*,
I liked it but of course they got the spacecraft all wrong.

Roger
I don't now if I could live with the possibility of sudden
death always hanging over me.

Nell
Paul hasn't asked any of his questions yet.

Paul
How can you deal with the risk that Bob lives with?

Bob
Good question.

Nell
I can't.

Judy
You needn't have answered that.

Nell
I wanted to say it.

Judy
What kind of thing are you going to write?

Paul
It'll be a piece of fiction.
(*To* **Nell**.) I promise I won't quote you or portray you.

Nell
Why have you come to talk to us then?

Paul
It's research.

Bob
Do you use a computer?

Paul
No, I write directly on paper.

Bob
Hard work?

Paul
There aren't many words in a play,
so the work's not in writing them down
but in thinking them up.

7

Alex *and* **Stone**.

Alex
Is there something else I can do now?

Stone
What else could anyone do?

Alex
No, you misunderstand; I just want a job.

Stone
This is your job now: to be what you are, for life.

Alex
What do I do?

Stone
We want to observe you
and we need to use you.
You want to further our work don't you?

Alex
How can I live like this?
Everywhere I go people smile at me.
There are no strangers any more.

Stone
Relax, all these people love you.
You belong to them now.

Alex
But have I changed?
Or has the world changed?
Is it everyone else that's changed?

Stone
You've see things no one else has seen.
They imagine you must know things no one else knows.
I shouldn't dwell on it.

Alex
You know how if you repeat a word endlessly
it becomes nonsense?
I've repeated my story so many times
it has become meaningless.

Stone
Why should you have to talk?

Alex
Why should I have to talk?

Stone
There's no need for you to speak directly to the press ever
again.
I can get a writer to write speeches for you.

Alex
Good.
If I didn't have to speak life would be easier.

Stone
You can write your autobiography now.

Alex
But I am so young.

Stone
It needn't be long.

Alex
How can I write a book about an hour in space?

Stone
Everyone wants to know about you.

Alex
What is there to tell?
My childhood was like any other.

Stone
You once said your father, when he was a child,
ran seven miles just to see an aeroplane land.

Alex
Yes, it's true.

Stone
That would be a good place to start.

Alex
Before I was born?

Stone
People will be inspired to know that you had a childhood like
any other.
Everything that ever happened to you is significant now,
in retrospect.
Think about that.

Alex
I can't write.

Stone
I'll get a writer who can write your autobiography
and your speeches.

Alex
Why did you pick me?

Stone
Why do you ask that question,

when you know the answer?
Don't you?

Alex
I'm sorry.

Stone
I understand that you are human.

8

Nell
If you could speak out
and tell people who you were
you might expect to be understood
but who would listen?

When they selected the first non-astronaut
to go into space
they chose a teacher
because teachers are trained communicators.

NASA was looking for the person
who could do the best job of describing
the experience of being on the shuttle
to the most people on earth.

Ten finalists were picked
from twelve thousand applicants
and when they announced the one
who was to fly on the Challenger,
I was at the White House:
we were guests for the day.

By chance
we were trapped in an elevator
with all ten candidates,
and I noticed the name of the manufacturer
because it was a company
who built parts of the Challenger itself.

She was standing next to me
the girl they chose;
a social historian

who had developed a course in the American Woman.
Now each of the teachers had a different project
so while we waited
for the repair men
she explained her idea.
It was simple.

It was to write a journal of the space flight,
no one had attempted that before.
'I believe history should be told in the words
of the common people,'
she said.

9

Anna *and* **Alex**.

Anna
Did you get a new job?

Alex
No but I don't have to speak any more.
A writer is going to write my speeches
and my autobiography.

Anna
People are only interested in what you did.
They forget we lived before
and have to live afterwards too.
Did you ask for more money?

Alex
No.

Anna
You are too generous with yourself.

Alex
Don't be mercenary.
We have a lot more now;
we don't want.

Anna
You forget how we lived.
You forget the ice on the inside of the window.

Alex
Don't you see there's more to this?

Anna
What other purpose could there be
than the betterment of our lives?
Isn't that what's behind it all?
Isn't that what this is about?

Alex
I don't know.
I've seen things no one else has seen,
I know things no one else knows
and somehow I have to live with it.
Can you imagine what that's like?

Anna
Yes.

Alex
Recently when I've told people,
I wonder they believe it.
It hardly seems true to me any more.

Anna
When you first came back and told me
I knew it was true then.

Alex
The words and experiences were close together.
I think the first time you say something it's real;
after that it becomes a story.

Anna
You have no reason to bear this alone.
Is there anything left you haven't told?

Alex
Only you and I will ever know?

Anna
Is this something I wouldn't expect to hear?

Alex
Light passed through my head, in space.

Anna
Did you close your eyes?
Everyone sees light when they close their eyes.

Alex
It went right in through my head!
In here, behind my forehead
there were flickers of light in here.

Anna
No wonder you didn't tell anyone.

Alex
What do you think it was?

Anna
Lightning?

Alex
That would be painful.
I felt no pain at all.

Anna
Has it affected your mind?
Have there been any after-effects?

Alex
No but perhaps they'll discover something when they dissect
my brain?

Anna
If it's brain damage you'll need treatment
before the autopsy stage.

Alex
How would you feel if I was shown to be a fake?

Anna
We'd lose everything
but as far as I am concerned you'd be the same person.

Alex
I think even if there's damage
no one could tell I was aware.
Now, even if I can't do anything else:
by not speaking
I shall exist as myself again

rather than only as what I did.
No one will know what I haven't told
and life will be more straightforward.

Anna
Until it happens again.

Alex
To me?

Anna
To others,
on other flights
in the future.
What if someone else gets light passing though their head?

Alex
What can I do?

Anna
You have to hope your experience was unique.

10

In the restaurant. As 6: **Nell**, **Bob**, **Roger**, **Paul** *and* **Judy**. **Nell**
and **Bob** *talk aside while* **Roger** *lectures* **Paul** *and* **Judy** *watches.*

Nell
What other horrors are there?

Bob
I wanted to protect you from that.

Nell
Too late, now it's time I knew everything.

Roger
Have you got an idea of the scale of the Universe?
Here's a way of thinking of it:
everyone sees the moon, you can imagine how far that is.
If this piece of paper, the thickness of it,
stands for the distance to the moon,
how tall would the stack be
to represent the distance to the sun?

Nell
This matters to you more than life itself doesn't it?

Paul *is listening to* **Nell** *and* **Bob**.

Roger (*to* **Paul**)
How tall would it be?

Bob (*to* **Nell**)
I know I am blessed you see.

Paul
Let me think about that.

Nell (*to* **Bob**)
I need to know of these dangers.

Bob
I don't know everything.

Nell
What am I being protected from?

Bob
It's me that's at risk.

Roger (*to* **Paul**)
Yes?

Nell (*to* **Bob**)
You rely on my support
yet you keep me in ignorance of your true situation?

Paul (*to* **Roger**)
Tell me.

Roger
It would be ninety miles high.

Nell (*to* **Bob**)
Am I to hide my concern from you?

Roger
Now search further in your mind
to the heart of the galaxy
within which our solar system exists.
If the thickness of this paper
stands for the distance to the moon,

how tall would the stack be
to represent the distance to the centre of the Milky Way?

Nell (*to* **Bob**)
How can you know you are blessed?

Roger (*to* **Paul**)
Well?

Paul
What?

Bob *exits to go to the Gents*.

Roger
Are you listening?

Judy
It would stretch from here to the sun.

Roger
That's the right answer.
Who told you that?

Paul
Does that make you feel insignificant?

Roger
No, not when it's me that's saying it.

Judy *takes* **Nell** *aside*.

Judy
Can you give me a lift home?

Nell
Yes, let's get out of here.

Judy
If we don't leave now
we'll become the subject of this.

Nell
Did I say too much?

Judy
How do you know he won't quote you?

Nell
I am not an astronaut am I?

Judy
You realise my husband's just 'playing up to camera'.

Nell
Was that what Bob did?

Roger
People say they can't imagine
an edge to the Universe
but when you look at the night sky
some of the light that reaches your eye
came from the edge of the Universe.
It started travelling at the beginning of time
and meets your eye tonight.

Paul
You mean the eye can see further
than the mind can stretch?

Nell
I feel sick.

Judy
I'm a doctor.

Nell
Do you think Bob wants to die?
I know I could get over it if he didn't come back.

Judy
How can you know that?

Nell
It would be easier than this.

Judy
You only think that.

Nell
He built a window in the kitchen ceiling
so that I shouldn't forget him in orbit
then I saw him falling through it in a burning space suit.

Judy
A day-dream.

Nell
How can I live with my imagination
when I discover the facts are worse?

Paul (*to* **Roger**)
I can try to imagine an edge to the Universe
but there's always going to be space beyond isn't there?

Roger
No, I know that the Universe is finite
because the night sky is dark;
if it were infinite then the sky would be bright
with the light of infinite stars
wouldn't it?

Bob *returns.*

Judy
We're leaving you to talk.

Bob
I'll come, let's all go now.

Nell
No, you can fucking stay and answer the questions.

Judy (*to* **Roger**)
You can see us to the car.

Paul
Good night.

Judy *and* **Nell** *exit with* **Roger**.

Bob
I can't stay long.

Paul
He's tactless isn't he?

Bob
I'm used to blunt questions.
At least he didn't ask how the cost can be justified
when people are starving.

Paul
What is it you do exactly?

Bob
I'm the pilot.
My job is to land the space shuttle,
the wings enable it to glide down onto a runway
but as there's no engine,
there's no chance of flying round again
so I have to get it right, first time, each time.

Paul
How can you do that?

Bob
It's skill. I am the best pilot.

Paul
In what way best?

Bob
I'm kidding you.
We have a computer.
I am a technician.

Roger *has returned.*

Roger
Why don't they land with parachutes,
like they used to,
then the shuttle wouldn't need wings?

Bob
He's right, the wings are the source of all the trouble.
They stress the whole craft and make launching
problematic as the Challenger showed.

Paul
Why does it have wings then?

Roger
They need your keys, they're waiting outside.

Bob
The shuttle needs wings so it can land after a single orbit.

Paul
Why?

Bob
This was part of the original brief from Congress . . .

Roger
Keys!

Bob
So it could drop a bomb
and land without passing over again.

Roger
Shall I drop your keys out to her?

Bob
No, I'll go, I'll take them both home.
It's no problem.

Bob *exits.*

Paul
You drove him away.
Did you need to hammer him with questions?

Roger
I want to know what it's like.

Paul
Remember I'm the one that's doing research here.

Roger
I suggested this dinner.

Paul *takes the bill.*

Paul
How shall we pay this?

Roger
You have the grant.

Paul
The more I learn the less I can imagine
who would want to be an astronaut.

Roger
I can.
If you are an astronomer
eventually you get the urge to stick your head
out into the Universe itself.
Perhaps I'll find what I'm looking for that way?

Paul
You think you have a chance?
This is something you mean to do?

Judy *re-enters but* **Roger** *does not notice.*

Roger
It's what's most important to me,
becoming an astronaut and getting into space.

Paul *sees* **Judy.**

Paul
What about your wife?
How does she fit into this?

Roger
She asks if I'd give up my work for her sake!

Judy *hits* **Roger.**

Judy
Bob's car won't start,
we all have to go now.

11

Bob
I was born in the most affluent nation on earth.
A secure home filled me with confidence.
As a young man my ambition was encouraged
but I never felt the need to be competitive.
I was always first at whatever I did.

When I applied to join the corps
they showed me ink blots.
To me they always looked the same.
Always the same part of the female anatomy.
I knew I couldn't say that each time
so I had to find other images.

A volcano. A horse's head.
A forest reflected in water. An iceberg.
A butterfly. The Milky Way.
Deep sea creatures.

Some people look and find oblivion,
patches of doubt merging to block out the light.
You can fall head first through the paper
out of yourself and into madness.

When I said,
'The shape on the paper is the shape of the Milky Way,'
the psychiatrist told me
that the ancients believed the Milky Way
was the path between Heaven and Earth.
Isn't that neat? I got the job.

And so,
speaking for myself:
because no car hit me in the street,
because the cancer did not bite,
because my parents met at all,
and I am here:

how can I not know that I am blessed?

12

Anna *and* **Alex**. **Bob** *and* **Paul**. *These two dialogues exist
independent of each other.*

Anna (*reads from a book entitled 'Look to the Sky'*)
'You must envisage the earth beneath you, very blue, more
blue than you could imagine and all the colours vivid and
bright. No photograph can show the brightness of these
colours. The earth is turning. The light of the sun illuminates
everything against the dark of space but when the earth
obscures the sun then you are in the black itself with only
stars; and the bulk of the earth shows as darkness where
there's no star.'

Alex
When I hear that I am there.

Bob
Truth ought to be more exciting than fiction
but there's been a big failure of communication.

People are more interested in sci-fi
than the reality of what we do,
that's why we had Disney build us a visitor centre here.

Paul
Thanks for agreeing to talk more.
After last night I wondered if you'd care to see me again.

Bob
We need people to understand what we do now,
that's why we're all keen to do what we can to help you.

Paul
Can I go to a launch?

Bob
Sure, we'll get a schedule and you can pick a flight.

Paul
I'll come to yours.

Bob
OK.

Anna
Are these your words?
Have you even read your autobiography?

Alex
I wasn't interested in what he wrote
but I'll read it if there's more like that.

Anna
What does it say about me in here?
I didn't meet this writer.
What does he know about me?

Bob
Would you like to go into space yourself?

Paul
Me, frankly I'd rather burn in hell;
but on the other hand, if I got the chance to go I'd go.

Bob
They've always wanted to send a writer

or an artist of some kind,
someone who could communicate the experience through art.

Paul
That's what I am doing here.

Bob
We thought a musician or a composer would be best and
they proposed the singer John Denver
but then the whole idea was abandoned after Challenger.

Alex
What does it matter if the whole thing is invented?
Let people believe what they choose.

Anna
It means I don't exist.

Alex
You exist.
You live and breathe and have thoughts don't you?
I'm telling you you exist.

Anna
Yes but not in there.

Paul
When it's so dangerous why are people
still going into space?

Bob
Listen, some people will tell you there's a one-in-six chance
of the shuttle exploding each time it flies
but if it had to be entirely safe
no one could ever go into space
(or walk down the street for that matter).
No one is asked to be an astronaut but plenty want to do it.

Anna (*reads again*)
'I shared with her my dream of flight.'
It was me who dreamed of flight.

Alex
Some dream of yours?
Most people don't even recall their dreams.

Anna
Did you tell him?

Alex
He did research.

Anna
Where does this all come from?

Alex
His imagination, where else?

Paul
Let me ask you something.
When you first went into space·
what surprised you?

Bob
Nothing. There were no surprises.

Paul
Nothing? What about the flaws in the shuttle itself?

Bob
(Usually those are only discovered afterwards.)
No, we have very good training,
we simulate each mission many times:
we want to minimise the challenge to an astronaut.

Anna
So this is fiction!

Alex
Neither of us exists then: I am not in it either.

Anna
It's your autobiography! It says what you did.

Alex
He consulted the technicians

to write an account of operating the craft
when I didn't do anything.

Paul
You insulate yourself against the experience?

Bob
We aim to eliminate the unknown.
In each simulation we test the crew
with some unexpected event
and they have to deal with it,
so that when it comes to going into space for real
it's a relief there are no surprises.
Sometimes people say it's less exciting than the simulation.

Anna
Everyone knows what you did.

Alex
What I did?
I saw. I ate. I took pictures.
Apart from that it happened to me.
I was simply there.
I sat there.
I could only look.

Anna
You had controls.

Alex
Automatic. I couldn't touch them.
Only in an emergency would they have given me the code to
unlock them.

Paul
So tell me about this failure of communication?

Bob
Congress needs a reason to let us do this,
once it was military expediency:
we demonstrated our superior technology to the world

but the end of the Cold War was a great loss,
now the Space Race is finished
and the thing itself isn't enough of a reason.

Anna
No one knows that you didn't do anything.

Alex
What am I if I didn't do anything:
the pilot or the passenger?
Perhaps it could have been anyone?

Anna
It couldn't have been me.

Alex
What shall I do?
If there's not this then there isn't anything.

Anna
You're alive.

Alex
So?

Anna
You're not allowed to complain.
You were the first man in space.

Bob
What's happened: I see it like the discovery of fire
or the invention of language.

People's indifference puzzles me.

What went wrong?
Has the media failed us?
Or is it that no one believed it from the start?

I always thought everyone wants to think
they live at a significant time; and we do.
This is where there's been a failure,
no one understands it for itself.

Paul
You know, you've been an astronaut.
How can someone else?

Bob
I'm hoping your play will help us with that.
And now that I'm inviting you to a launch
I'm also hoping you'll ignore what my wife said last night.

Anna
What is the value of all this
if no one is to know what it's really like?

Alex
Perhaps you're asking for the impossible?

Anna
But I know.

Alex
Or do you *think* you know?

Anna
What do *you* know?

Alex
You forget, the object was simply to send a man
and bring him back safely.
I've done all that is required of me.
I just have to remain healthy,
pulse normal, breathing regular:
show how unaffected I am by this experience.

Anna
Unless you are affected you could be a stand-in for yourself.

Paul
Are you telling me it's all over,
the manned exploration of space?

Bob
Where is there to go?
There's plenty of space out there
but it's all too far away.

Paul
You've been lucky then?

Bob
Two flights in the last ten years
and another coming up.
I am one of the favoured few.

Alex
I've done my best.
I am not a poet or a philosopher.
The achievement consists in the act not in the telling.

Anna
You owe it to us all.

Alex
What do I owe?
I've told all I could tell.

Anna
Aren't you forgetting something?

Alex
I'm sure I've forgotten most of it now
apart from what I could never put into words,
and no one can take that from me.
I must have something to hold on to.
The experience was mine alone,
I risked my life for it.
My vision.

Anna
Your vision?
My dream.

Paul
And what did you learn?

Bob
I saw the change:
the planet has turned from blue to grey in ten years.

Paul
That must have been a surprise?

Bob
Yes.

13

Alex, **Dan** *and* **Carl**.

Alex
No?

Dan
That day I was glad not to be chosen.

Carl
None of us wanted to be chosen but you.

Alex
We competed like dogs!

Dan
I was happy to be the standby.

Alex
So you both lied.

Carl
None of us could have admitted this then.

Alex
Why are you telling me?

Dan
We felt a duty to square with you now.

Alex
Don't you trust the machinery?

Carl
No, I know you can trust a machine
in a way you can never trust a person.

Dan
It's easy to have faith now
but it seemed remote then.

I was sick when they launched the rocket.
Between us here, I don't know if I could have kept my mind.

Alex
Have no fear of madness,
it's just a question of keeping a sense of proportion.
I had no disturbance.
My mind was clear the whole time.
You don't change.
Everything is the same.
It's simply that everyone thinks you've changed.

Carl
Thanks to you,
I am happy to be next, we both are.

Alex
What if you had been chosen first?

Carl
It's clear now that you were the only possible choice then.
None of us understood the source of your courage.
The way you spoke that day, it was philosophical.
We didn't recognise what we heard.

Alex
What did I say?

Dan
I've read your book over and over;
the bit about your childhood,
it was just like mine.

Alex
Weren't all our childhoods the same?

Carl
And yet we are different people.

Dan
I've already imagined myself in space,
reading that.

Alex
No you haven't.

Dan
No, why?

Alex
Because it is more incredible than you could imagine.

Dan
Then, when I am there for real I shall see it with your eyes.

Carl
Surely the best part must be being able to tell the story
afterwards?

Dan
If I had done what you did I could die happy.
You need do nothing more, need you?

Alex
You must realise I didn't write that book?
I don't even know how I was chosen.
And I never understood why he said he wasn't being
generous.

Carl
That was in case you never came back.

Alex
It was a complete unknown.
In those hours before the flight
I was at peace with myself,
weren't we all prepared to die?

Carl
Perhaps you know how to die
but I don't want to sacrifice my life.

Alex
Scared?

Dan
It's only the moment of death that I dread.

Carl
I may not fear it but I don't invite it either;
for the sake of those I love,
I think of what my absence would subject them to.

Dan
If you died up there
you would orbit the earth for ever.

Alex
That would be immortality.

Carl
How did you say goodbye to your wife?

Enter **Stone**.

Alex
Quickly.

Stone
The day we met and I chose the first of you,
what was possible became actual then through his belief;
he staked his life on it.
Now this isn't just a possibility any more.
Here are copies of the photo we took that day.
Take them back to your families.
Let them see the courage and confidence in those faces.

That day, it was inevitable that some would be disappointed
but I kept my word and now you two are next.

Alex
I've told them all there is to know.

Stone
I can see you've no fear.

Carl
It's natural to feel concern where there's risk
but I know luck is on our side.

Dan
I feel only anticipation.
I mean to look so carefully, take in all I can.

Alex
But remember you are not paid to look.

Stone
Are you prepared to stake your lives?

Carl
We have his example.
We're ready.

Dan
Yes. I know what's going to happen.
We have a job to do.

Stone
Good.
The word from above has always been
that this can continue as long as I can guarantee success;
this man achieved 100 per cent success,
what he said was always exactly what we wanted to hear.

Alex
When my father was a child
he ran seven miles just to see an aeroplane land.

Stone
Often I think of the future that we shall never see. I could
easily go mad when I try to imagine what will happen that I
shall not know but then I think we were the first and in that
far distant future they will look back and wonder what it was
like for us in the beginning which is something they'll never
know. Then I remember what good fortune I have to be here
now.

Alex
Your genius remains a mystery to us all.

Stone
There's no mystery to a single-track mind.
Once upon a time
I shot field-mice into the air
attached to sky rockets,
they lived and I never looked back.

Dan
Can I ask a question?
(*To* **Alex**.) Your autobiography *Look to the Sky*.
Did you call it that?

Stone
It was what he said that day:

'Everyone looks to the sky.'
Why did you say it?

Alex
I was just trying the words out.

Stone
We have thirty-six hours now,
you must first go and say goodbye to your families.

14

Oliver, **Gina** and **Paul**. **Gina** and **Paul** are looking at the moon.

Oliver (*aside*)
I am not Neil.
It could have been me
but it wasn't.
I was disappointed then
now I get fifty letters a day,
still.
I was not the first there
but I saw what he saw
I did what he did.

I saw the rockets blow up too,
I was one of that original group
but I didn't get to fly
until years later.

No doubt you've heard stories
about the men who walked on the moon.
People will tell you we're all crazy now
but then
I took that famous photograph
of the whole earth from space
and someone even claimed it as evidence
that the earth was indeed flat.

Gina (*aside to* **Paul**)
I persuaded him to meet you
and you should know that you are honoured
because he rarely talks about it.

Paul
Well thanks, I'm down here for the launch
so this works out well for me.

Gina
It's a pleasure,
it's an excuse for me to get him talking.

On a clear night we often come out here
and watch the moon as an alternative to television.

Paul
Tonight it looks as if you could reach out and touch it.

Gina
I've touched it, with these fingers;
a piece of the moon is available for all
at the Air and Space Museum in Washington.

Paul
What is it like, is it just a rock?

Gina
No, it's beautiful,
the caress of a million fingers
has smoothed it to the consistency of polished steel.

Oliver *joins them.*

Oliver (*to* **Paul**)
You spoke to Alan Bean?

Paul
Yes.

Oliver
Nobody hassles Alan.

Paul
So I found.

Oliver
Did you call Neil?

Paul
No. I was told it would be a waste of time.

Oliver
He's not eloquent.

Paul
Tell me about being on the moon.

Oliver
When I was there I could stretch out my thumb
and cover up the earth.

Paul
That small?

Oliver
From a quarter of a million miles away
our fragile earth is the only coloured thing,
the moon is grey or biscuit brown
and space is black.
I'll show you where I was.
Do you see the areas of light on the surface?

Paul
Yes.

Oliver
The lower one to the left,
it's called the Sea of Clouds
(a wilderness without a footprint),
that's it,
that's where I was,
that's where I walked on the moon.
Can you see it?

Paul
Yes.

Oliver
I can't.

Paul
No.

Oliver
It's just a blur to me now.
It was a long time ago,
my eyesight isn't what it was
and I left my glasses inside.

Paul
I remember clearly

watching it on television
when I was a child.

Oliver
There are two places in my mind:
one is the close-up moon where I was
and this out-of-focus one up in the sky is another.

Gina
People look at the moon
and they see a light in the sky.
I had to look and tell myself: it has no light,
it does not wax and wane,
what I see is what's lit by the sun.

Oliver
She sees only what she believes.

Gina
If you believed what you saw
you'd think the moon gave its own light.

Paul (*to* **Oliver**)
And if you believed what you saw
you might think there was a blur in the sky?

Oliver
Yes, isn't it the way we perceive things
that makes them what they are?

15

Carl
I fear weakness
so I did not question.
I mistook anger for cowardice
when I am no coward:
I let anger take my voice away.

I got this chance
and took it
though I do not trust it.
I am a gambler
because I am lucky

and I got the chance
that's why I took it:
it was a gift.

Looks at the photo.

What kind of chance do I have?
Who will remember me?
Shall I get to tell the story afterwards?
I am one of the other people in this photograph.
I mistook anger for cowardice
when I am no coward,
I let anger take my voice away:
I said goodbye to my wife quickly.

What did we want?
What shall I find?
Expectation is all I have left.
It's not weakness that I fear,
I've learnt I am no coward.

16

Judy *and* **Nell**.

Judy
Speak your mind.

Nell
Part of me wants to kick,
part of me wants to yell,
part of me wants to kill.

Judy
I understand that.
I would be the same.

Nell
When we married I said to him
'I'm going to put you first in my life,
will you put me first in yours?'
Big mistake.
He expects my support and encouragement

while he intends to fly as many times as he can.
That's what he lives for really.

Judy
What about your needs?

Nell
Forget it. I do everything myself.
I mow the lawn, take out the garbage,
keep the home and family in order.
That's my contribution to the US effort in space.

Judy
This is no good for you.

Nell
It takes the skin off me like sandpaper.
At the Cape
I'll watch the NASA channel,
the kids will visit Seaworld
and for what anybody knows
we may never see him again.

Judy
You must confront him.
This demeans you.

Nell
Even the pay's no good,
he doesn't get much more than a standard pilot's wage,
I have to work.
When he doesn't fly the shuttle any more
the rewards are plenty and waiting.
Any number of companies want to have an astronaut's name
on the notepaper.
There are professorships too, even admin jobs.
(They pay the managers a lot more than the astronauts.)

Judy
You can't wait for that.
It may never happen.

Nell
I've accepted he may die.

Judy
What then?

Nell
That night,
the night we had dinner
I did confront him then.

Judy
Did he tell you he did it for you?

Nell
No, and he didn't say he couldn't do it without me.

Judy
So?

Nell
I don't hate him.

Judy
I don't understand how anyone could tolerate this.

Nell
I went out onto the lawn
and stood in the sprinkler to cool off!
I watched our family each in their separate rooms
then I lay down in the wet
and looked up into the dark.

Judy
I don't understand you.

Nell
I have no self-pity.
I know;
because of all I imagine,
even after what I've learnt;
that in his situation,
if I was him,
if I were to get the opportunity
I would take it:
I would do the same.
Wouldn't you?

Wouldn't anyone?
Wouldn't you?

Judy *does not answer but takes* **Nell** *in her arms.*

17

Stone *and* **Alex**.

Stone *(aside)*
If you have a strong idea
then you don't listen to others
because you can't afford that time
and there will always be those who disagree.

That's why I am so organised
because I don't mean to waste any time:
I work every second of the day.

You only have so many years
and I intend to use all my time
because I need to know that I lived.

Alex
You worked your whole life for this.
Why did you give it away?

Stone
I've got you.

Alex
Why not go yourself?
Why choose someone else?

Stone
The importance of an enterprise of this kind
cannot rest in any individual alone
so even if it were practical
it couldn't be me.
I knew I should never be the one.

Alex
How do I deserve this?
Why me?
I need to hear you say it.

Stone
I wanted someone with aspiration
but without doubts.

Alex
Out of all of us, only me then.
How did you tell?

Stone
What?
Why are you staring?
Have you got doubts now?

Alex
Why am I unable to do anything else?

Stone
Is something wrong?
You're well are you?
Perhaps you need a check-up.
Not drinking too much?

Alex
I've still got hopes that's all.

Stone
In life we learn to accept.
No one avoids getting old.
Ambition is something:
you could get more money;
I can give you more authority
but you refuse.
Why not find some concrete ambitions for yourself?
Abandon hope in the abstract.

Alex
I am allowed hopes.

Stone
Don't be sentimental.
Do you think I could have done what I've done through
hope.

Alex
I need hope.

Stone
I know you want to go back.
I can't imagine how it can be
to see that only once.

Alex
That's not it.

Stone
There might be a virtue in sending you again
to prove a man can do it.
But I can't take that risk.
I can't risk you now.

Alex
You talk of 100 per cent success.
You can never guarantee it will work!
This is Russian roulette:
you pull the trigger once
and it doesn't go off
so you pull the trigger again.

Stone
You're not talking rationally now.
You don't know who you are.
Ambition is something,
hopes can destroy a man.

Stone *exits*.

Alex
Being alone in space,
more alone than anyone's ever been;
I was entirely myself,
I knew where I was
and why I was there.

I looked out
and thought:
life evolved on earth,
creatures emerged from the slime
and eventually
there's me here.

In the deep silence
I heard my body working,

my heart beating,
the blood pulsing.

Then I saw my face
reflected in the glass
and noticed my teeth
how savage they look;
I've got teeth like an animal.
They're my least human bit.

Three billion people on earth.

Teeth are for biting.
My body is pulsing with hot blood
and my head is full of darkness.

18

As 14: **Paul**, **Oliver**, **Gina**.

Paul (*to* **Oliver**)
What happened to you exactly?
Is there a word for it?

Oliver
It was wonder.

Paul
Wonder?

Oliver
I was changed by it. Afterwards
I had to piece together a new world for myself,
everything had been taken away from me.

Gina
There he was trying to solve the riddle of existence
and not a penny to his name.

Paul
Surely, as an astronaut, the bank gave you credit?

Oliver
They kept my cheques for the signatures
when I first came back from the moon.

Gina
He had to make his own money to live.

Oliver
I had no money.

Gina
People think he made a lot of money
out of going to the moon.
What do you think he got?
Guess.

Paul
Tell me.

Oliver
It cost them six times my weight in gold to put me there.

Gina
What he got was thirty dollars,
in travel expenses: the moon and back.
Can you beat it?
No one could live on that.
He had to find his own living.

Paul
When you came back from the moon
how do you decide how to spend the rest of your life?

Oliver
I had to find a way to live.

Paul
Surely you could have got a job?

Gina
He was in no state to do a job at that time.

Oliver
I was shaken up.
It was an exceptional situation:
I knew I still had many years of my life in front of me.
I had to work out how to spend them.
I had to earn a living.
So I asked myself how I liked to spend time.

But where do you start?
What was I going to do?
You are wasting your time unless you can find something.
I could have done anything.
My first marriage ended then
but I wasn't going to lay down and die,
I told myself:
'You have nothing to lose.'
That's how it was when I came back from the moon.

Paul
You're not telling me what you're telling me.

Oliver
Are you a goal-orientated person?

Paul
I'm writing this play.

Oliver
I was a goal-orientated person
but I fulfilled my aspiration in one shot.
It was a morbid kind of freedom.
When you have been changed you can never go back
though life can get you down
but I know I have had my moment of ecstasy.

Gina
When we first met,
we were introduced and we shook hands.
'Hey,' I thought,
'I just touched a man who walked on the moon.'
What a feeling!
I was so aware of it
my hand seemed to swell to fill the whole room.
Then we married
and I got to touch him all over.

Paul
What's it like being married to a man who walked on the moon?

Gina
I don't compete with him

but I am not in his shadow either.
When we got your letter
I wanted to meet you
because I've worked in the theatre too,
I am an actor.
When people see me
they hear only the lines I speak
and see only the role I play
but it isn't me. Not who I am.
That's how we came to understand each other.
Our situations are parallel.
People know him for what he did
but it isn't who he is.

Paul (*to* **Oliver**)
Who are you?

Oliver
Excuse me?
What is the question?

Paul
Did you find how to live?
You've obviously got a life here.

Oliver
I found a way to live.
I realised that what I suffered wasn't unique,
and that I could help others in similar situations.
So I set up an organisation to do it.
In fact so many Americans have a problem making contact
with reality
that we're the fastest-growing institute here in the States
now.

Gina (*to* **Paul**)
When you've done the research,
who's going to write your script?

Paul
Who? Me.

Gina
Haven't you got a ghost?

Paul
No? I'll write it.

Oliver
We know a lot of people who've done books
but I never met anyone who actually wrote one before.

Paul
So this is a first for both of us?

They shake hands. **Paul** *looks at his hand and then up at the moon.*

Gina (*aside*)
And I thought
what did he learn from that?
Did you see what got across?

Paul *exits.*

Who was he?
We never heard from him again;
perhaps it was a hoax?

Everyone wants to feel touched by it.

Fifteen years
since I married the man in the moon.
A lot changes.
For a start
every particle of your body is replaced
each seven years.
Neither of us is who we were
in any sense.

Our youngest child,
what do you think she asks me
all the time?
'What shall I do next?'

There's the pool
we jump in and out of it
all day.

This is an incredible place
where we live here
you cut the grass
and it just grows right up again.

19

Stone *and* **Anna**.

Stone
I need your help.
There's a problem.
I don't know if we can get them back alive.

Anna
Can't you do anything?

Stone
Nothing can be done until there's contact.
If we can establish a signal,
if any kind of communication is possible
an alarm bell will ring in here.
Until that happens I can only wait.
Your husband has gone to inform the families.
Logically, I know you must have some understanding
of what they may suffer.
We don't know what will happen
but they need to remain positive.
In the meantime
I'm keen they shouldn't talk to anyone else.
I need your help.
Will you go to them and stay with them?

Anna
I'll do all I can for them.

Stone
I'm grateful to you.
You'll see your husband there.
(I've got a car coming to pick you up in a few minutes.)

Anna
Before I go
in this moment now
I've got something to ask,
there's something I want to know,
about him.

Stone
What?

Anna
In confidence?

Stone
Yes.

Anna
Why did you choose him?

Stone
He is the best pilot.

Anna
I know the controls were automatic.

Stone
In an emergency
we'd have given him the code to unlock them.

Anna
A pilot with no function.

Stone
He's a brave man.

Anna
I'm proud of him.

Stone
He's modest about what he did.

Anna
It could have been an ape.

Stone
No, he is a man
he has the mind of a man,
we wanted to send him
and return him safely.

Anna
To see if he could stand it?

Stone
He carried it off so well
that I've begun to believe
that perhaps any adult
could be capable of this.

Anna
Anyone at all?

Stone
If they were healthy,
even a woman: though women's minds are weaker
and the bodies stranger.

Anna
I've no doubt you could find a strong woman
with a mind of her own.

Stone
It was a difficult choice we had the first time.
We had to choose someone
if it hadn't been him it would have been another.

Anna
But you did choose.
How did you choose?

Stone
We wanted a representative response.

Anna
Is representative like average?

Stone
None of them had an unusual intelligence or imagination.
He was average.

Anna
He thinks he is the best pilot.

Stone
They were all top pilots in different ways.
We didn't want to choose anyone who was exceptional within
the confines of the group.
He was the least distinctive.

Anna
Ordinary.

Stone
Yes, shouldn't that be enough for anyone?
Doesn't it reflect well on him

that an ordinary man did this?
There's no shame in it is there?

Anna
I won't tell him.

Stone
Why do you need to know this?
Have there been after-effects?
Is he holding anything to himself?

Anna
No.

Stone
Is there a domestic problem?
Has he changed?

Anna
No. He says I treat him differently now,
but then, I learnt he was prepared to say goodbye to me
for the sake of this.

Stone
You resent it?

Anna
No. I discovered that I exist independent of him.

Stone
These are harsh words.

Anna
When I met him, he was already a pilot,
I had never been in a plane.

Stone
Are you jealous?

Anna
No. I wouldn't choose this.

Stone
You prefer the domestic world?

Anna
We had aspirations and dreams
but we were small-minded

(I asked him if he had seen God),
and we were poor.
I never knew there were so many countries in the world until
we visited them all.

Stone
Why doesn't the car come?
I need you to go now.

Anna
How do you manage to look innocent
when you are so guilty?

Stone
Responsible
but not guilty.
People have died when bridges collapse
but bridges are still built.

Anna
What will happen to these men?
How will they die?

Stone
If we didn't continue
then the sacrifices of thousands of engineers
who worked for this would be in vain.
At the end of the war they would have closed this place down
but I said I could create something here,
if I have achieved anything
it is that I took the missiles I designed then
and turned them to a peaceful use now.

Anna
But why? Why?
Tell me why.

Stone
Have you any idea of the pain this causes me?

Alex *has entered,* **Stone** *sees him.*

Stone
I told you you had no reason to be grateful

and you have no reason to be ungrateful either.
I was neither generous nor ungenerous to you.
You chose to put yourself forward and you were chosen.

Alex
I wish I was an exceptional person
or had something unique to say.

Stone
What did you expect: transformation?
(*Aside.*) Why?
What is this question?
Why?
What does it mean?
WHY?

Alarm bell rings.

20

Paul *and* **Sylvie.**

Paul (*reads from a book*)
'Eight years after his epoch-making first spaceflight Gagarin
was killed when the plane he was piloting crashed on a
routine flight. Rumour and conjecture have gathered around
this event. If it was suicide no one can ascribe a motive,
equally no one can explain how such an *exceptional* pilot could
make such a tragic error.'

Sylvie
How is that relevant?

Paul
The American experience cannot be the whole story.

Sylvie
Isn't this about us,
what you're doing?

Paul
How could I write about you?
What do I know about you?

Sylvie
Why the fuck are you here then?
What have you learnt?

Paul
I've no conclusion
but my hands are dirty now,
I'm culpable.

Sylvie
You can't evade having an opinion.

Paul
I'll choose what I write
just as you can choose what you tell me.
I wanted to speak to some astronauts here,
and cosmonauts in Russia,
find out what the experience was in common, OK?

Sylvie
I've been thinking about your question
'What is it like in space?'

Paul
Yes.

Sylvie
There are several questions there.

You are asking how does it feel,
what is the experience of being there?
What *is* it like?

You are asking what kind of environment
what kind of place is it?
What is *it* like?

You are asking to compare the experience
with another experience.
What *is* it 'like'?

You are asking to compare the environment
with another environment.
What is *it* 'like'?

My answer was the answer only to the first question.
'What *is* it like?'

Paul
'More incredible than you could imagine.'
Give me some other answers.
What is *it* like?

Sylvie
Space is empty.
Empty space.

Paul
What *is* it 'like?'

Sylvie
What is *it* 'like?'
These questions have the same answer.
It is unlike anything.
There is an absence of all that's familiar.

Paul
I was told the training was designed to eliminate the
unknown.
Someone told me there were no surprises.
'More incredible than you could imagine'?
By that token every experience is a surprise.
It doesn't mean anything does it?
It's bullshit.

Sylvie
Yeah. You can say that
but when everything is full of wonder
why should we let it become mundane?

For fifteen years the astronauts colluded
to conceal the existence of flicker flashes,
the micro-meteorites that pass through the brain in space.

They are small enough to enter and exit through the walls of
the craft and we only know they exist because they create a
sensation of light when they pass through the retina.

This was experienced from the start
but no one dared admit it because it seemed too strange.

Paul
Why did you say you had no imagination?

Sylvie
Because we need to deal only in reality
when our lives are on the line.
When that rocket goes today
a charge equivalent to the entire national grid
will be in one place at one moment.

Paul
Why did you choose to become an astronaut?
Tell me honestly.
There must be a personal reason.

Sylvie
Perhaps it was
because I always dreamed of flight?
As I'm sure you're aware
it is one of the most common female fantasies.

Paul
How would I know that?

Sylvie
We're of an age (I imagine)
I was born in '61
the first year of spaceflight;
for me, this is what happened in our lives.
I wanted to be at the centre of it.
That's why I am here.

Paul
And you still feel you are ordinary?

Sylvie
The population of the earth is over five billion now,
who cannot feel that?

Paul
Do you think I've been wasting your time?

Sylvie
I am one of the standby crew today.
I've nothing else to do.
It was my decision.
I did choose to speak to you.

Paul
I am an interloper.
Why should you trust me?

Sylvie
When I see your play
then I'll find out the truth.

21

Paul
No one dares expect what will happen
when they see a rocket go.

At ignition there's light
many times stronger than the sun.
Nothing prepares you for it,
no one warns you.
The image stays on the eye.

You expect a sound.
There is no sound
until it hits you like a kick in the chest
and the air splits apart
with the force of cast iron breaking.

The shuttle barely moves.

Slowly it leaves the earth.

Paul *begins to rise into the air.*

You pray it will work.

You watch until there's just the light
and then
in a moment
that's gone too.

You realise: it went through the roof of the sky.

Then
you look again
and you see
only a trace

of white smoke
in the form
of
a
question mark,
hanging in the air.

Paul *plunges upwards into the blue, tearing the sky as if it were
paper and vanishing from sight. The sky falls away and the Universe
is revealed in which the earth spins revealed only by points of light on
the surface. Then the light of the sun illuminates the whole planet and
passes over, giving a sequence of night to day and back to night.*

Afterword

A Playwright's Research

I touched the moon, touched it with the hand that writes these words. What moved me wasn't that the rock came from the moon but that millions of fingers had imparted a metallic sheen to its surface, reflecting a meaning and importance delivered by the attention of all those people. Thanks to NASA the fulfilment of this aspiration is now open to everyone at the Air and Space Museum in Washington, where they keep the only piece of the moon on earth that's available for the public touch.

Imagine my discomfort when I met my first astronaut and as they walked into the room I discovered in that instant that I didn't believe it, knew it, yes, but believed it barely. My doubts surfaced as I explored the Lyndon Johnson Space Center in Houston where astronauts are trained. As I walked the hundred yards' length of the Saturn V rocket laid out on the grass, its primitivism appalled me, like an early steam engine in a museum, all the welds were visible and the words painted on by a signwriter. Its first fifteen feet comprised the capsule for the people and the rest was simply a canister of fuel, stood on end and lit. Passing from the rocket I came across one of capsules, expecting the sleekness of mass-produced technology instead I found scuffed pieces of metal riveted together and interlaced with a tangle of wires. The space suits were hand-stitched in places. Running my hand along the outside of the tiny capsule burnt to the colour of ashes, pitted and scored by the furnace temperature of the earth's atmosphere, I could scarcely comprehend how this do-it-yourself enterprise had worked.

Next I went to see the moon rocks in their storage building constructed to withstand all natural disasters and nuclear explosions too. The enigmatic stones are kept in pure nitrogen, to prevent rusting, within transparent boxes. From behind bullet-proof glass in the viewing facility I scrutinised these intractable pieces of granite. They were cherished like babies in incubators except these weren't alive, they were dead rocks.

Once I overcame my disbelief I was assaulted by the irony

in the choice of the most rational individuals in order to propel them into the mysterious. At first it was frustratingly difficult to get any sense at all from the astronauts of what it was like. I was beginning to realise that there probably weren't answers to some of my questions, and I recognised a powerful desire to experience some of this wonder for myself.

I arrived in Cape Canaveral during the spring break. One road runs parallel to the ocean and the motels that fill the space between were riddled with spring breakers: students partying, drinking and frantically coupling. Four days until the launch of the space shuttle Atlantis. The surfing stores had shelves of launch souvenirs, tariff boards carried good luck messages to the crew and each hotel reception had its display of signed astronaut photographs. It was a relief to escape an English April and be in the Florida sunshine. I got an astronaut haircut.

The launch was scheduled for 8 a.m. At 5 a.m. when I climbed into my taxi it was raining. The freeway was already busy and the driver explained it would reach a standstill within an hour. Several hundred thousand people drive overnight across country to see each launch.

At the gates to the space centre I was assigned a security guard who escorted me to the press compound. We drove along a causeway through a swamp, oranges hung in the dark undergrowth of dawn and ditches on either side had notices: BEWARE THIS DRAINAGE DITCH IS INFESTED WITH POISONOUS SNAKES. My driver told me the story of the jealous astronaut who killed a six-foot snake, placed it under the desk of a colleague moon-bound with the next Apollo mission, and then telephoned to summon him to his desk for a joke.

The press room is an eighty-foot dome with desks in concentric circles. I staked out a space between 'Newsweek' and 'Scientific American' chalking the words 'Royal National Theatre' on the desk label. Thousands of pigeon-holes line the outer wall of the building, in each one a different press release. Most of the newsmen were watching the astronauts suiting up on close circuit TV. Once I'd acquired a pile of literature I went outside in search of action.

Overshadowing everything stands the VAB (Vehicle Assembly Building) the biggest building in the world, they claim. In here it's possible to construct a Saturn V rocket and wheel it out on end. Beneath this grey monolith sits Mission Control. To my right was a primitive stadium built of steel girders, behind it the tent for sponsors and on my left were the TV vans. Straight ahead was the digital clock, each side of a digit the length of a fluorescent tube, and behind it half a mile away across the lake was the space shuttle. TV crews were preparing their stake-outs, with shuttle in left distance, immaculate news readers stood on wet grass practising their reports.

I walked past the great big clock down to the lakeside to see if the alligators were stirring yet. Rain flecked the sky. Pelicans circled over me but the lake dwellers did not show, like the shuttle they were waiting for the sun. I could only speculate at the emotions of those who gathered here to watch Apollo 11 launch the first men to the moon in 1969 or the space shuttle Challenger that took its crew of seven to their deaths in 1986 when a booster rocket exploded.

After several hours in the stadium reading NASA press releases I began to get excited by the countdown. With less than an hour to go the rhythm of the digital clock seemed to penetrate the air. The rain stopped. At ten minutes the launch was held for five to allow the clouds to clear. High-flying jets reported a launch window approaching.

When the countdown resumed everyone came out onto the lawn. The launch was going ahead. It was a curious social event, the crowd standing silent looking to the horizon. A minute to go. The launch pad was as still as it ever was. Then as if planned, there was a gap in the clouds exactly overhead. Ten seconds to go and a charge travelled through the crowd. We all counted in unison. At two seconds, clouds of smoke swelled from under the shuttle. Zero, and nothing happened. It doesn't fly right up into the air like a rocket should!

Nothing happened and I held my breath. The tiny white shuttle in the distance vibrated with a violence I cannot describe. It didn't ascend though. I was thinking why is there no sound? Why doesn't it move? I watched it for a couple of seconds just clear of the horizon, still vibrating and then the shock hit me. Palm trees struck the ground. I learnt why the stadium is made only of girders and the alligators got their morning call. Journalists and photographers were stumbling and staggering. Still the shuttle was barely above the horizon.

The shuttle rose in a gentle spiral trailing a delicate plume of smoke. A cloud bank took it from us at the moment the booster rockets were jettisoned and when it reappeared we were simply watching a bright light up in the sky. Then it was gone as if through a ceiling. We are used to seeing aeroplanes fly away and diminish but this vanishing seemed to surprise everyone. People exchanged comments and several rubbed their necks and then they all began to drift in the direction of breakfast in the NASA canteen. As the crowd moved faces turned back at the sky. I looked as well, just to check it had really gone. In the press room a TV monitor was showing the launch view from the inside of the shuttle: Cape Canaveral receding, then azure sky blending to cerulean and then the darkness of space.

When I returned in less than an hour a winking light on an illuminated map of the world revealed that the shuttle had orbited the earth in less than the time it took to eat my breakfast. Already it was off across the Atlantic for the second time that morning.

The day was the thirtieth anniversary of the flight of Yuri Gagarin. President Kennedy's encouragement of the Apollo programme was a response to the Russian space initiative. Bluntly, both competitors in the space race wanted to prove they had the best rockets and could nuke the other first if necessary. It wasn't peace that took men to the moon, this race was a central but incidental contest in the Cold War.

How was I to know if all I had learnt wasn't simply the American experience? Four days later I sat in a hotel room and choked with relief to watch the shuttle land safely. If I wanted to isolate the experience itself I needed to learn what was common among astronauts and cosmonauts in both countries. I switched the television off and decided to go to Russia and hear the other story.

By chance I picked the month that the Soviet Union collapsed, December 1991. Dina and Arkady, two editors of *Theatre* magazine were my hosts. They arranged a place for me to stay in a block on the outskirts of Moscow and introduced me to interpreters.

In Moscow, at the Exhibition of Economic Achievements in the Space Dome I had the privilege to attend the first rave to be held in the former USSR. THE YURI GAGARIN PARTY, held on his birthday, which was perhaps a mere pretext to use the Space Dome. The Space Dome is where they display the spacecraft and Gagarin's capsule was suspended above the crowd, just visible through the smoke, lasers and moving projections of his smiling face. Arkady and I stood among the heaving masses. He had visited the exhibition once before as a child and young communist pioneer. Overcome with the emotion of the moment he exclaimed 'This is the end of the Soviet Union!' He was right. The exhibition space is now a used-car lot.

At Star City on the outskirts of Moscow where they train cosmonauts, I visited the replica of Gagarin's office. Here is his diary open at the day his plane crashed. Today the cosmonauts come and sign their names in it before each flight. There's been no adequate explanation of his early death. I even heard a rumour that he was still alive somewhere in a remote Soviet mental institution. Perhaps the authorities killed him, wary of his international reputation and fearing he could speak out? Perhaps it was simply an accident? Or perhaps it was suicide? I asked myself why the first man in space should wish to kill himself.

Gagarin's body is in the Kremlin Wall on Red Square. He's almost the only figure from the communist era for whom young Russians have any respect. If it's possible to imagine a time when the names of Lenin and Stalin are forgotten then in that time surely people will come here to the place where Yuri Gagarin lies.

Westerners had only been admitted to Star City a few months previously. There were still people who had worked here in the early days. They told me that before Gagarin's flight almost no one but the chief engineer and Gagarin himself believed it could work. I was excited to meet cosmonauts, though they were more excited to meet me when they heard I had bottles of vodka. I tried to set up a visit to a launch in Baikonur from where they propelled Gagarin into space but circumstances conspired against me. Only later did I discover that Kazakhstan where the launch facility is situated was declaring itself independent of the Soviet Union at that moment.

At the Russian Academy of Science, I had the pleasure to spend some time with Svetlana Savitskaya, the second woman in space and the first to do a space walk. Shortly after Gagarin the Russians put a woman in space to prove it could be done. This woman, Valentina Tereshkova had been selected for her politically appropriate background and had a mirror attached to her space suit to check her make-up in space. When high temperature and air pressure caused her to pass out in orbit she was accused of falling asleep and no other woman got to be a cosmonaut for many years until Svetlana overcame the resistance.

She was fourteen when she saw Valentina's flight and decided then to do it herself. She practised gymnastics at school until she made the Olympic team. In further education she studied astronomy and engineering, she joined the college flying corps and achieved a pilot's licence to aerobatic standard. Next she applied to join the space programme and though they were not taking women they were forced to accept her as she was more qualified than any man. But they didn't forgive her for her independent womanhood.

This was the first time men and women had been together in space and when they returned to earth the technicians asked the men 'Did you fuck her?' 'Svetlana!' they replied, 'You must be joking!' I don't wish to imply that this misogyny is unique to the Russians because it was not until much later, in the early eighties, that the Americans chose to put a woman in space. Twelve middle-aged white men were sent to the moon.

On my last day the mission controller at Star City asked me if it would help me with my play to speak to the men orbiting on the space station Mir. These cosmonauts had recently been informed that the Soviet Union was over, that it was uncertain when they could return to earth and now they were asked to speak to a playwright from the Royal National Theatre in London. As I spoke to these men they completed half an orbit of the earth. Now I no longer doubted the reality of it.

For a brief spell when I returned I was proud to tell people they'd never meet anyone who knew as many astronauts as I did. From several quarters I encountered the urban myth of the mad astronauts: 'They're all crazy now aren't they?' I quickly learnt to keep my mouth shut or I'd be groping for words in response to the question that has no simple answer: 'What are they like?'

Methuen Contemporary Dramatists
include

Peter Barnes (three volumes)
Sebastian Barry
Edward Bond (six volumes)
Howard Brenton
 (two volumes)
Richard Cameron
Jim Cartwright
Caryl Churchill (two volumes)
Sarah Daniels (two volumes)
David Edgar (three volumes)
Dario Fo (two volumes)
Michael Frayn (two volumes)
Peter Handke
Jonathan Harvey
Declan Hughes
Terry Johnson
Bernard-Marie Koltès
Doug Lucie
David Mamet (three volumes)

Anthony Minghella
 (two volumes)
Tom Murphy (four volumes)
Phyllis Nagy
Peter Nichols (two volumes)
Philip Osment
Louise Page
Stephen Poliakoff
 (three volumes)
Christina Reid
Philip Ridley
Willy Russell
Ntozake Shange
Sam Shepard (two volumes)
David Storey (three volumes)
Sue Townsend
Michel Vinaver (two volumes)
Michael Wilcox

Methuen World Classics
include

Jean Anouilh (two volumes)
John Arden (two volumes)
Arden & D'Arcy
Brendan Behan
Aphra Behn
Bertolt Brecht (six volumes)
Büchner
Bulgakov
Calderón
Anton Chekhov
Noël Coward (five volumes)
Eduardo De Filippo
Max Frisch
Gorky
Harley Granville Barker
   (two volumes)
Henrik Ibsen (six volumes)
Lorca (three volumes)
Marivaux

Mustapha Matura
David Mercer (two volumes)
Arthur Miller (five volumes)
Molière
Musset
Clifford Odets
Joe Orton
A. W. Pinero
Luigi Pirandello
Terence Rattigan
W. Somerset Maugham
   (two volumes)
Wole Soyinka
August Strindberg
   (three volumes)
J. M. Synge
Ramón del Valle-Inclán
Frank Wedekind
Oscar Wilde

A SELECTED LIST OF
METHUEN MODERN PLAYS

☐ CLOSER	Patrick Marber	£6.99
☐ THE BEAUTY QUEEN OF LEENANE	Martin McDonagh	£6.99
☐ A SKULL IN CONNEMARA	Martin McDonagh	£6.99
☐ THE LONESOME WEST	Martin McDonagh	£6.99
☐ THE CRIPPLE OF INISHMAAN	Martin McDonagh	£6.99
☐ THE STEWARD OF CHRISTENDOM	Sebastian Barry	£6.99
☐ SHOPPING AND F***ING	Mark Ravenhill	£6.99
☐ FAUST (FAUST IS DEAD)	Mark Ravenhill	£5.99
☐ POLYGRAPH	Robert Lepage and Marie Brassard	£6.99
☐ BEAUTIFUL THING	Jonathan Harvey	£6.99
☐ MEMORY OF WATER & FIVE KINDS OF SILENCE	Shelagh Stephenson	£7.99
☐ WISHBONES	Lucinda Coxon	£6.99
☐ BONDAGERS & THE STRAW CHAIR	Sue Glover	£9.99
☐ SOME VOICES & PALE HORSE	Joe Penhall	£7.99
☐ KNIVES IN HENS	David Harrower	£6.99
☐ BOYS' LIFE & SEARCH AND DESTROY	Howard Korder	£8.99
☐ THE LIGHTS	Howard Korder	£6.99
☐ SERVING IT UP & A WEEK WITH TONY	David Eldridge	£8.99
☐ INSIDE TRADING	Malcolm Bradbury	£6.99
☐ MASTERCLASS	Terrence McNally	£5.99
☐ EUROPE & THE ARCHITECT	David Grieg	£7.99
☐ BLUE MURDER	Peter Nichols	£6.99
☐ BLASTED & PHAEDRA'S LOVE	Sarah Kane	£7.99

* All Methuen Drama books are available through mail order or from your local bookshop.

Please send cheque/eurocheque/postal order (sterling only) Access, Visa, Mastercard, Diners Card, Switch or Amex.

☐☐☐☐☐☐☐☐☐☐☐☐☐☐☐☐

Expiry Date: _____ Signature: _____

Please allow 75 pence per book for post and packing U.K.
Overseas customers please allow £1.00 per copy for post and packing.

ALL ORDERS TO:

Methuen Books, Books by Post, TBS Limited, The Book Service, Colchester Road, Frating Green, Colchester, Essex CO7 7DW.

NAME: _____

ADDRESS: _____

_____

_____

Please allow 28 days for delivery. Please tick box if you do not wish to receive any additional information ☐

Prices and availability subject to change without notice.